TRADITION MATTERS

●

Tradition Matters

MODERN GAÚCHO IDENTITY
IN BRAZIL

RUBEN OLIVEN

Translated by Carmen Chaves Tesser

•

COLUMBIA UNIVERSITY PRESS
NEW YORK

Columbia University Press
New York   Chichester, West Sussex

Copyright © 1996 Ruben Oliven
All rights reserved

A Parte e o Todo: A Diversidade Cultural no Brasil-Nação © 1992
Editora Vozes Ltda., Brazil

Library of Congress Cataloging-in-Publication Data

Oliven, Ruben George, 1945–
  [Parte e o todo. English]
  Tradition matters : modern Gaúcho identity in Brazil / Ruben Oliven ; translated by
Carmen Chaves Tesser.
      p.   cm.
  Includes bibliographical references and index.
  ISBN 0-231-10425-1 (pbk. : alk. paper)
  1. National characteristics, Brazilian.   2. Pluralism (Social sciences)—Brazil.
3. Gauchos—Brazil—Rio Grande do Sul.   4. Rio Grande do Sul (Brazil)—Civilization.
I. Title.
F2510.04213   1996
306'.0981—dc20   95-49668
                                                                              CIP

Printed in the United States of America
p 10 9 8 7 6 5 4 3 2 1

FOR DÉBORA

●

CONTENTS

Contents

ILLUSTRATIONS

Attempt to Proclaim the Federal Republic of the Gaúcho Pampa, 22–23 May 1993

1. Separatists prepare the scene.
2. Separatists wearing *bombachas* and boots carrying the flag of the Federal Republic of the Gaúcho Pampa.
3. The curious gather in the central square of Santa Cruz do Sul, where the Federal Republic of the Gaúcho Pampa was to be proclaimed.
4. Separatists with the flag of the Pampa Republic.
5. Separatists, the curious, and journalists.
6. Identification Card for the Federal Republic of the Gaúcho Pampa with the photograph of its creator, Irton Marx.

Gaúcho Characters

7. Gaúcho in the *Campanha* region (bordering Argentina).
8. Gaúchos in a small bar in the *Campanha* region.
9. A traditionalist musician who lives in the state's capital, Porto Alegre.

10. A couple of tourists from São Paulo visiting the California of Rio Grande do Sul Native Song Festival.

11. Camp in the California of Rio Grande do Sul Native Song Festival.

12. Stage for the presentation of the California of Rio Grande do Sul Native Song, featuring some musicians performing.

13. A student of Gaúcho music playing the accordion in a show in Porto Alegre.

14. A young man performing a Gaúcho dance in a traditional barbecue restaurant in Porto Alegre.

INTRODUCTION

A popular Brazilian song describes Brazil as "a tropical country, blessed by God and beautiful by nature." The lyrics picture, in a very familiar way, a well-known manner of representing Brazil—one that places the exotic in a central position. I do not wish to disagree with such a poetic metaphor; however, at the very least, one must be aware that a significant part of the Brazilian territory is outside the Tropics. This is the case of Rio Grande do Sul, the southernmost state in Brazil and one that cannot be represented as tropical. This state is often seen as the nonexotic part of Brazil, featuring a strong European presence and, at times, having more similarity with areas in Argentina and Uruguay, its bordering countries. All this indicates that there are different ways of belonging to a country the size of Brazil, in which not everything is beach, samba, and carnival.

Rio Grande do Sul has always had special characteristics because of its location, its colonization, and its history. In the past the state was an area of intense dispute between Portugal and Spain. Throughout its history the state has had a long tradition of wars and conflicts that lasted well into the era after Brazil's independence in 1822. One of these conflicts, the Farroupilha Revolution that began in 1835, had as its origin a lack of satisfaction with the excessive political and economic centralization imposed by the Brazilian Empire. The revolutionaries, who fought for ten years, succeeded in proclaiming an independent republic in 1836, and only after assuring themselves of amnesty did they sign a peace treaty with the imperial government. But the republic proclaimed by the revolutionaries continues as a figurative presence even today in the flag of Rio Grande do Sul. In this flag one finds featured not only the republic's name, Rio Grandian Republic, and the date of the deflagration of the Farroupilha Revolution, 20 September 1835, but also its motto, "Liberty, Equality, and Humanity," assuring a place for the episode in the collective memory of the inhabitants of the state.

The inhabitants of Rio Grande do Sul consider themselves Brazilian by choice, and they like to emphasize their individuality regarding the rest of Brazil. In the social construction of their identity, they use elements that refer to a glorious past, one dominated by the figure of the Gaúcho, a word that initially meant a vagabond and cattle thief but later came to mean the farm hand and warrior always associated with the figure of the horseman. Today, the word is a patronymic for the citizen of the state of Rio Grande do Sul.

Since the decade of the 1930s, Brazil has experienced a growing economic, political, and administrative centralization that has brought about a weakening of regional and state powers. This process became accentuated after 1964, when the military took over power and promoted a greater integration of the national market and the implantation of networks of roads, telecommunications, mass communication, and so on. With these measures, regional and state powers weakened even more.

However, in spite of—or perhaps because of—this growing centralization, one can observe today in Brazil certain tendencies that are in opposition to it and that manifest themselves by emphasizing many needs, such as those for a true federalism, for the affirmation of the advantages of an administrative decentralization, for a tributary reform that would give more resources to states and municipalities, and for the affirmation of regional and state identities that make salient the issue of Brazilian diversity. Among these regional identities is that of Rio Grande do Sul, a state in which we find a strong revival of Gaúcho culture.

At the end of the decade of the 1970s it was common to hear that Gaúcho tradition was an endangered species or that it was reduced to pockets of tradition and folklore. After all, Brazil was taking huge steps toward integrating itself. The military government that took power in 1964 promoted a conservative modernization, meaning a gradual political and economic centralization. This meant, among other things, that Brazilian television, with its prime-time soap operas watched by millions of people, began to reach a growing number of homes and began to promote a culture that seemed increasingly to be the national culture. Considering that Rio Grande do Sul had become an industrialized state in which a large majority of the population is urban, it was thought that there was no space within its culture for the rural and equestrian figure of the Gaúcho.

The end of the 1970s and the beginning of the 1980s were marked by the process of *abertura* [opening] in which the Brazilian civil society organized itself and began to pressure the government toward a democratization of the regime. As new political spaces were conquered, different political actors appeared and new social identities were created. It came as a surprise to many that the organization of the civil society occurred not only at the level of parties and labor unions but also at the level of social movements, of groups that fought for specific issues and which up until then did not have a great part within the Brazilian stage: voices came from feminist groups, from homosexuals, from "green" movements, from movements concerned with price increases, from religious movements, and so on.

It is in this context of the clamoring for a voice that we find the revival of "Gauchism." Throughout the eighties one notices an intense growth of interest toward things linked to Rio Grande do Sul. With the spread of the Centers for Gaúcho Tradition throughout the state, as well as in other states and countries where Gaúchos migrated, there appeared a new interest in festivals of Gaúcho music, rodeos, television and radio programs, newspaper articles, books and specialized publishing houses, restaurants, and so on. This points to a new market for symbolic and material goods that involves a great number of people and is expanding. A large part of this market is formed by middle-class young people in the cities who would probably fall off a horse if they tried to ride one. It is also interesting that a new field of intellectual debate developed and that within it different actors appeared wishing to speak on behalf of Gaúcho tradition.

In the beginning of the Gaúcho revival, some intellectuals saw in this phenomenon a passing fancy or an obsolete ideology. The phenomenon proved to be lasting, and it is difficult to imagine that an ideology can be simultaneously effective and anachronistic.

To understand this phenomenon does not mean merely to capture a process that is occurring in a specific state in Brazil. It means also to understand two other phenomena. The first has to do with regional and cultural differences in a country that has continental dimensions and where there always was a certain difficulty in understanding and accepting differences. The second phenomenon has to do with processes that are occurring at the global level and that deal with the collapse of some countries and the appearance of new ones, processes that point toward the renewed importance of the meaning of national identity at the end of the twentieth century. Until recently it was frequently imagined that this was a concept about to lose its importance considering the process of cultural globalization and of growing economic internationalization. What has been shown is that precisely because of these processes, what is national (and what is regional) acquired a new prominence that appears in a series of conflicts in Europe as well as in less developed continents. Tradition is a key variable in these processes.

This book tries to show precisely how modernity re-creates tradition. The study was organized to guide the reader from the realm of theory to that of fieldwork. Thus the first chapter delineates the book's theoretical framework. The chapter discusses the issue of the revival of tradition and that of national and regional feelings at the end of a century when the world is seen more and more as a global village. In this chapter I argue that as the world becomes a more global village, and as economies become more transnational and Western Europe becomes more unified, the themes of nationalism and regionalism return to the forefront with a doubled impetus in several places in the world. In this process, tradition has a marked presence and constitutes a background of movements that are linked to the construction of different social identities.

Chapters 2 to 5 discuss this phenomenon in relation to Brazil. In the second chapter I develop the relationship between the national and the regional in the construction of Brazilian identity. I point to the fact that these questions are brought up to date as new social contexts are created. I examine the recurrence of these themes during a period that goes from the time of the Proclamation of the Brazilian Republic in 1889 until today. I argue that throughout this period questions posited again and again are those of a strong central government versus a federation of states, nation versus region, unity versus diversity, national versus foreign, popular versus erudite, tradition versus modernity, and so on.

Chapters 3, 4, and 5 take Rio Grande do Sul as a case study to discuss the questions previously analyzed. In the third chapter I attempt to demonstrate how the relationship between Rio Grande do Sul and Brazil is marked by the tension between autonomy and integration. The state can be seen as a case of regionalism constantly being evoked, brought up to date and posited in new situations that are historical, economic, and political. However, although the junctures may differ and the rules of the discourse may be modernized, the basic substrata on which they rest is surprisingly similar. The idea of emphasizing the state's peculiarities while simultaneously affirming its belonging to Brazil constitutes one of the main foundations of the Gaúcho social identity that is projected from the past to the present, always informing action and creating present practices.

In the fourth chapter I analyze the Gaúcho Traditionalist Movement (GTM), which claims to be the largest popular culture movement in the Western world, with two million active participants. The first center for Gaúcho traditions, the *35 Centro de Tradições Gaúchas*, created in 1948 in Porto Alegre by secondary school students from the pastoral areas of Rio Grande do Sul, serves as a model to the approximately one thousand traditionalist entities that cover all the regions in the state. The traditionalist values spread by its members are founded in the country life of the regions of cattle latifundia. The representation of the figure of the Gaúcho also served as a model for the colonists of German and Italian origin in the areas of minifundia where there never was a large pastoral complex. The representation also served as a model for those who left Rio Grande do Sul and went to Santa Catarina, Paraná, and Mato Grosso do Sul, and other Brazilian states, where they created centers for Gaúcho traditions. Rio Grandians who went to live abroad created centers for Gaúcho traditions in cities such as Los Angeles and Osaka, Japan.

The expansion of a movement that spreads tradition based on a rural culture of the pastoral region that has lost its hegemony in a predominantly urban state poses the question of the social construction of the Gaúcho identity—the theme of the fifth chapter. On examining the model that is built when one speaks of Gaúcho things, I show that the model is based both in a past that existed in the pastoral region of the *Campanha* located in the southwest of Rio Grande do Sul as well as in the real or idealized figure of the Gaúcho himself. I also analyze how and why the 1980s were marked by a growing revival of activities linked to Gaúcho traditions and how the Gaúcho identity transformed itself into an element of dispute. Although they tried to position themselves in opposite camps, the principal contenders—the *traditionalists* and the *nativists*—were both arguing around the same semantic field: the figure of the Gaúcho, the means of constructing it, the criteria for defining its authenticity, the instances of its legitimacy and its consecration, and so on.

What occurs in Rio Grande do Sul seems to indicate that nowadays one can only reach what is national through what is regional; that is, for Rio Grandians it is only possible to be Brazilian if they are Gaúcho first. Gaúcho identity today is posed not only in terms of the Farroupilha tradition, but also as an expression of cultural difference in a country where mass communication tends to homogenize society in a cultural way through patterns that often originate in the beaches of southern Rio de Janeiro.

In the last chapter I review the themes developed in the book and try to argue some of the recent phenomena that are occurring in Brazil and in the world at the turn of this century. I contend that the process of cultural globalization points to the present day value of the issue of diversity.

The research that served as a basis for this book was carried out in the Graduate Program in Social Anthropology of the Federal University of Rio Grande do Sul (UFRGS), where I am a professor. I received support from this university, from the CNPQ (National Council for Scientific Development), and from FAPERGS (Research Foundation of the State of Rio Grande do Sul).

My colleagues in the Graduate Program in Social Anthropology at UFRGS—Ari Pedro Oro, Claudia Fonseca, Ondina Fachel Leal, and Sérgio Alves Teixeira—read parts or all of the manuscript and gave me extremely valuable suggestions for which I am very grateful. I presented and discussed parts of this work at various academic meetings in Brazil and abroad. In the United States, at the University of California, Berkeley, where I was a Visiting Professor in the Department of Anthropology from August 1993 to December 1994, I had the opportunity to discuss my research with professors and students, which proved to be an enriching experience.

Students majoring in the social sciences at UFRGS who participated at different times as research assistants and carried out vital tasks were Alberto Groisman, Adriana de Mello Boff, Andrea Daniella Lamas Cardarello, Léo Voigt, Flávia Rieth, Daniel Riva Knauth, José Antônio Pires de Miranda, Miguel Benjamin Minguillo Neto, Andréa Fachel Leal, and Antonádia Monteiro Borges.

The majority of the photographs in this book were taken by Luiz Eduardo Achutti, my former student and presently a professor of photography at the Federal University of Rio Grande do Sul. Andréa Fachel Leal, research assistant, took some of the photographs of the attempt to proclaim the Republic of the Gaúcho Pampa. The design of the book's cover and the photograph on it is credited to Roberto Silva. Airton Bittencourt, a geography student at the Federal University of Rio Grande do Sul, developed the maps that are included in the book.

Several people linked to Gaúcho themes agreed to speak to me and helped me with precious material and information. Their contribution was fundamental to the development of this book, and I am grateful.

Arabela read a good portion of this work and was, as always, my key interlocutor.

I had the honor of receiving, in 1993, the José Albertino Rodrigues Prize for the Best Book of the Year given by the Brazilian Association for Research and Graduate Studies in Social Sciences for this book, published originally in Brazil by Editora Vozes and entitled *A Parte e o Todo: a diversidade cultural no Brasil-Nação*.

Carmen Chaves Tesser, Professor of Romance Languages at the University of Georgia, translated the book from Portuguese into English. Her strong linguistic competence, combined with her solid knowledge of Brazilian and Rio Grandian history, made it possible for me to recognize myself in the text translated into English.

TRADITION MATTERS

•

Chapter One

NATION AND TRADITION AT THE TURN OF THE MILLENNIUM

●

At the turn of a century during which mankind stepped on the moon, it may seem paradoxical to return once again to such issues as tradition and the national question. The twentieth century is marked as much by the ideal of socialist internationalization as it is by the shattering of the notion of separate countries, the latter achieved primarily through the action of multinational corporations.

It suffices, however, to look at a map of the world to ascertain the large number of societies—many of them very old and apparently quite stable—in which the issue of what is national is the order of the day, and where the fragmentations, frequently linked to cultural, ethnic, and regional identities, are strong. In large part, these fragmentations involve quite violent conflicts that have lasted for years and are far from being resolved.

Writing during the 1920s Marcel Mauss established a parallel between the modern nation and the primitive clan. His parallel is based on the symbols through which both types of societies are represented. To him, the nation is homogeneous like the primitive clan and supposedly composed of citizens who hold equal status. It has a flag as a symbol, just as the clan had its totem; it has its deity, the Fatherland, as the clan had its ancestral animal-gods. Just like the primitive tribe, the nation has its dialect elevated to the dignity of a language. The nation also has internal rights that contrast with international rights.[1]

A similar comparison had already been established by Emile Durkheim. While studying what he considered to be the most elementary form of religious life, he postulated that totemism would be, in the final analysis, a means by which the clan could worship itself; that is, the external and visible manner of worshiping a society by its members who, in this primitive phase, were not able to represent the sacred and complex character of their society by any means other than the emblem, the symbol, and the sign. Thus the totem, or the symbol that represents the clan, would be hypostatized and would become associated with security, well-being, and continuity. For this reason, Durkheim refers to the totem as "a flag; it is the sign by which each clan distinguishes itself from the others, the visible mark of its personality, a mark borne by everything which is part of the clan under any name whatsoever, men, beasts or things."[2]

Durkheim offers the example of a soldier who falls defending his flag and affirms that the soldier clearly did not believe that his self-sacrifice was done on behalf of a piece of cloth.[3] In fact, we know that the soldier who dies in battle believes he is giving his life for his country, symbolized by the flag, an emblem that in the end becomes more sacred than the reality it represents.[4]

Interpreting what he called "totemic illusion," Claude Lévi-Strauss demonstrated that totemic classifications serve to distinguish some men from others. Thus the differences among animals that man can extract from nature and transfer to the culture, "are adopted as emblems by groups of men in order to do away with their own resemblances."[5]

Roger C. Poole, in his reading of Lévi-Strauss, states that totemic classifications "are like what we call 'nationalism.' We call each nation by a semi-condescending nickname, which very often has to do with some animal or plant associated with that nation. Likewise, we might remember the example Durkheim gives of the soldier who dies for a flag. In the same way, the so-called primitive human being separates himself from his fellow man."[6]

Of course, when one compares a modern nation to a primitive clan, one runs the risk of producing what Mariza G. S. Peirano called "ethnocentrism in reverse," that is, thinking of complex societies as no more than simple societies that have been "complexified." Peirano argues that complex societies have their own historicity and that they are nation-states trying to integrate their different "parts" from the regional or territorial point of view as well as from the social point of view. Thus "nations or nation-states possess ideologies and usually present them as something very ancient, almost 'eternal and immortal.' These representations also suggest that nations are solidly integrated social formations."[7]

In reality, the concept of nation is a cultural product that emerges in Europe toward the end of the eighteenth century[8] and it comprises, according to Benedict Anderson, "an imagined political community."[9] In this process of historical construction, relationships between old and new, past and present, and tradition and modernity become a constant and take on a fundamental importance. If, as Max Weber posits, a nation "is a community of sentiment . . . which normally tends to produce a state of its own,"[10] one must invoke ancient traditions (real or invented) as the "natural" foundation for the national identity that is being created. These traditions tend to obscure the recent and historical characteristics of the nation-states.

Just as the nation-state tries to delimit and guard its geopolitical borders, it is also compelled to demarcate its cultural borders, establishing what does and does not belong to the nation. Through this process one builds a national identity which tries to create an image for the community that it includes. Ernest Gellner shows, however, that

> the cultural shreds and patches used by nationalism are often arbitrary historical inventions. Any old shred and patch would have served as well. But in no way does it follow that the principle of nationalism itself, as opposed to the avatars it happens to pick up for its incarnations, is itself in the least contingent and accidental. Nothing could be further from the truth than such a supposition. Nationalism is not what it seems, and above all it is not what it seems to itself. The cultures it claims to defend and

revive are often its own inventions, or are modified out of all recognition. Nonetheless the nationalistic principle as such, as distinct from each of its specific forms, and from the individually distinctive nonsense which it may preach, has very deep roots in our shared current condition, is not at all contingent, and will not easily be denied.[11]

The process of consolidation of the nation-states is extremely recent, even in societies that seem to be completely integrated today. Thus, for example, France was barely integrated until the eighteenth century at the time of "the kingdom, when it still remained a patchwork of regions rather than a unified nation until the Revolution and perhaps even well into the nineteenth century."[12]

There are even cases in which the same society is represented as if it were divided in two large antagonistic regions. Writing at the beginning of the century, Antonio Gramsci, in "The Southern Question," argued that the ideology disseminated to the masses through different kinds of bourgeois propaganda in Northern Italy was the following:

> It is well known what ideology is propagated through the multifarious forms of bourgeois propaganda among the masses of the North: the South is a lead weight which impedes a more rapid civil development of Italy; the southerners are biologically inferior beings, semi-barbarians or complete barbarians by natural destiny; if the South is backward, the fault is not to be found in the capitalist system or in any other historical cause, but it is the fault of nature which has made the southerner lazy, incapable, criminal, barbarous, moderating his stepmother's fate by purely individual outbursts of great geniuses, who are like solitary palms in an arid and sterile desert.[13]

In the Italian case, the differences between North and South are presented as if each owes its being fundamentally to biological causes, in a process through which one goes from the economic and societal sphere to that of nature as the explaining factor in the backwardness of a determined region. It is not difficult to capture how this eminently ideological operation has as its objective the desire to mask the real causes of inequalities between the two regions, which Gramsci associated very properly with economic and social factors that must be sought in the very history of Italy.

One of the uses that can be made for the regionalist claim is that of trying to oppose regions among themselves, presupposing that each one is internally homogeneous and therefore filled with common interests that conceal its fragmentations in the realms of the social, the economic, and the cultural. Regionalism points to the differences that exist among regions and utilizes these differences in the construction of self-identities. However, like nationalism, regionalism also encompasses different facets, frequently expressing positions of very different groups, containing issues stemming from popular claims to the masked interests of the dominant classes.

Therefore, in discussing the regional question at the beginning of this century in Peru, José Carlos Mariátegui, in a classical study, argued that regionalist aspirations were imprecise and undefined. They did not become concrete through categorical and vigorous claims. Regionalism would not be a movement in Peru nor would it be a current or a program, but merely a vague expression of discontentment and ill will. This way, the polemic between federalists and centralists was as obsolete as the controversy between conservatives and liberals. Federalism would not be, therefore, a popular claim, formulated by the indigenous masses, but rather a claim of the *gamonalismo*, whose preaching would be restricted to the limits of the small bourgeoisie of the old colonial cities. Thus, as centralism sought support from regional *caciquismo* and from *gamonalismo* (often prone to call themselves or feel like federalists), federalism would recruit its followers among the *caciques* or *gamonales* who had fallen from grace with the central power.

For this reason, for Mariátegui, decentralization alone, as a merely political and administrative reform, would not point to any form of progress in the sense of solving the "Indian problems" or the "land problem." On the contrary, decentralization whose single objective was to give regions or departments a somewhat ample autonomy would tend to increase the power of the *gamonalismo*, going against a solution based on the interests of the indigenous masses. This being the case, the author concludes that

> the regions and provinces are absolutely right to condemn centralism, its methods, and its institutions. They are also right to denounce an organization that concentrates the administration of the republic in the capital. But they are completely wrong when, deceived by a mirage, they believe that decentralization will suffice to solve their basic problems.[14]

Political connotations of regionalism vary, however, according to the social context and to the time in which they emerge. Analyzing France at the beginning of the 1980s, Michel Rocard, then a minister of state responsible for territorial planning, later the prime minister in the socialist government of President Mitterand, maintained that "today, all of the [French] Left is—daringly—regionalist."[15] Significantly, the regionalist option of the French Left was justified in the name of democracy, of efficiency, and of the search for cultural roots. Thus Rocard spoke of the recognition that unity was not to be confused with uniformity in the consciousness-raising of the "right to difference." To achieve a true democracy, decisions must be made as close as possible to those who will have to live with the decisions or feel their consequences, that is, in the department (French administrative unit), which is the most appropriate level to deal with social problems if one wishes to find a feeling of belonging beyond one's own parish, beyond one's own country.

How do we explain, then, that in certain contexts regionalism is considered a conservative posture whereas in others it carries a progressive banner? What is behind the regionalist claim?

One of the fundamental points of reference to clarify the question would certainly be the process of national unification that accompanies the formation of the state and which, besides centralizing power, has been shown to be historically contrary to the maintenance of cultural and regional diversity.

Discussing the phenomenon, Ann R. Markusen maintains that the understanding of the concepts of region and of regionalism is much more problematic than the definitions of categories such as state and class that refer in a nonambiguous way to social groups and hierarchies. Regionalism would be better associated with the emergence of the state and with a territorial configuration that the state assumed historically. A political dimension carries out a fundamental role in the definition of regionalism, for although a regional cause may be solely economic in nature, its objective is essentially political. A cause becomes regionalized precisely by means of a region putting forth a claim before a state institution. The regional cause has as its objective the changing of the way territorial issues are handled. Therefore, the state and its politics are central elements in the characterization of the phenomenon, since

"regionalism is a political claim of a group of people identified ter-
ritorially against one or many mechanisms of the State."[16]

Although she argues that in essence regionalism is not itself a
cultural phenomenon, Markusen suggests that in many cases it
must be researched within a middle ground in which cultural
forces may be an active component in the formation of regional disputes. She points out that cultural conflicts often coincide with
regional divisions and that many regional disputes are, at first, cultural in substance, at least at the conscious level:

> For example, although the division between Catholic and
> Protestant Ireland has its roots in the appropriation of Catholic
> lands by England as well as the occupation of these lands by
> troops loyal to the British crown, as time went on, the struggle
> for an independent Ireland took a decisively cultural tone that
> demanded the lifting of the restrictions on the use of the Gaelic
> language, on the practice of Catholicism, and on the imposed
> educational system.[17]

We therefore have a phenomenon that is essentially political in
its definition and that can also be characterized by social inequal-
ity, but one that is articulated by mobilizing collective feelings and
promoting identities and ideologies associated with social memory. Let us then proceed from the political and economic dimension to that of culture in which symbolism plays a predominant
part.

Regionalism in this perspective can be seen as a battleground in
which groups who hold different positions and interests face one
another. In this sense, Pierre Bourdieu argues that the battles for
regional identity are constituted as a particular case of fights for
classification, fights for the imposition of a legitimate definition of
a division of the social world. Therefore,

> regionalism (or nationalism) is nothing more than a particular in
> the properly symbolic battles in which the agents are engaged,
> whether individually and in a dispersed manner or collectively
> and in an organized fashion, and these agents have as their objec-
> tive the conservation or transformation of the relationship of
> symbolic forces and related interests—economic or symbolic
> ones; or, if one prefers, the conservation or transformation of the
> laws that govern the material or symbolic prizes attached to sym-

bolic manifestations (objectives or intentional ones) of social identity.[18]

In this process, the social construction of memory becomes of fundamental importance. Maurice Halbwachs, a disciple of Durkheim and one of the precursors of memory studies, demonstrated that personal memory is linked to group memory and that the latter, in turn, is linked to the collective memory of each society. We might call such collective memory a tradition. Since the nation was seen as the most complete form of a group, national memory would then represent the most complete form of a collective memory.[19]

Michael Pollack argues that, "in the tradition of Durkheim, emphasis is given to the quasi institutional force of this collective memory, its duration, its continuity, and its stability. Thus Halbwachs is far from seeing in this collective memory an imposition, a specific form of domination or of symbolic violence. What he does is accentuate the positive functions carried out through common memory. By this he means those functions that reinforce social cohesion, not through coercion but through the affective connection to the group; that is why he uses the term 'affective community.' "[20]

More recent studies have pointed precisely to how much the construction of a national memory and of a national identity, far from being a consensus, is linked to the groups that are seen as having power and legitimate authority so that they become guardians of memory. This process, which involves symbolic disputes, reaches the entire state by means of mass communication and through the intellectuals from the different groups in competition.

Collective memory is linked to a relatively restricted group that carries a tradition; it approximates myth and manifests itself through the ritualization of tradition. National memory refers to a larger and more generic entity (the nation), approximating more closely an ideology and therefore extending itself to society as a whole and defining itself as a universal: "Collective memory of popular groups is particular, while national memory is universal. Therefore, what is national cannot constitute itself as a continuum of popular values; it must constitute itself as a second-order discourse."[21]

There is a strong tendency in the human sciences to attribute a linearity to social dynamics. This tendency—which appears in several different forms such as the idea of evolution, the possibility of an unlimited progress, the idea of development, the issue of growing rationality, the concept of modernity—frequently comes face to face with evidence that contradicts it. British anthropologists in the last century got around this problem using the concept of *survivals*, a term coined by Edward Tylor when he referred to the cultural stages that would have been historically surpassed in the process of human evolution. Survivals would be the elements that were kept without a specific function since the conditions that gave them origin had disappeared and their original functions had gone through such major changes that their original meaning was gone.[22] Criticizing this notion, Eunice Ribeiro Durham argues that the verification of the persistence of traditional cultural patterns or the glorification of the past

> is not an explanation of any social phenomenon, but phenomena in themselves that must be explained in the analysis of the social transformation process. For many years, anthropologists destroyed the illusion of the explanatory value of the concept of survivals. Cultural patterns survived in as much as there is survival of the situations that gave them origin, or these cultural patterns altered their meaning to express new problems.[23]

Even though many anthropologists criticized this notion, claiming that if a cultural element "survives" it must accomplish some type of function, the notion is present, often by another name, in several analyses of cultural dynamics. Thus when ideologies are examined, their anachronism is frequently pointed out, in addition to their aspect of producing a false reality. It is as if an ideology, besides achieving the inversion of reality, does so through ideas that have been surpassed by time. However, inasmuch as an ideology is measured by its power to produce discourse that will have repercussions in the social imaginary, if a determined ideology is efficient in working with apparently obsolete notions, then the anachronism will be only in the mind of the researcher and not in the minds of social agents. An ideology is successful if it achieves the perception of unifying interests in the different social groups. For this to happen, it is necessary that a discourse, when addressing subjects, carry a verisimilar message, because "for an ideology to become such, 'to capture' its subjects, to bring about a loyalty, it is

necessary that the meanings produced by its discourse find an echo
in the imaginary of the individuals to whom it is directed; that is, it
is necessary that there be a certain amount of fit between the meanings of this discourse and the representations of the subjects."[24]

One of the phenomena that becomes salient when one deals
with this problematic is the marked presence of traditions in societies that consider themselves modern. It is common for countries
and regions engaged in modernizing transformations to emphasize
the value of the past and the necessity to venerate it. Likewise, at
the root of the construction of nations, it is necessary to point to a
real or imagined past that would give substance to the community
designated by this political form. The nation that wishes to be
modern and freed of the old religious and aristocratic social order is
forced to utilize tradition to justify itself. Thus the cult of tradition,
far from being anachronistic, is perfectly articulated with modernity and progress.

The evoking of tradition—understood as certain value-laden ori-
entations consecrated by the past—manifests itself frequently at
times of processes of social change, such as times of transition from
one type of society to another, times of crises, or loss of economic or
political power or both. At these times one studies folklore; traditions are even invented, as Eric Hobsbawm suggests. He distinguished between the traditions of modern societies and the customs
of traditional societies. The former are characterized by the invari-
ability and by the reference to the past (real or created) that imposes
fixed and generally formalized practices such as repetition. However,

> "custom" cannot afford to be invariant, because even in "tradi-
> tional" societies life is not so. Customary or common law still
> shows this combination of flexibility in substance and formal
> adherence to precedent. The difference between "tradition" and
> "custom" in our sense is indeed well illustrated here. "Custom"
> is what judges do, and "tradition" (in this instance invented tra-
> dition) is the wig, robe and other formal paraphernalia and ritu-
> alized practices surrounding their substantive actions. The
> decline of "custom" inevitably changes the "tradition" with
> which it is habitually intertwined.[25]

Hobsbawm further argues that, "in spite of much invention,
new traditions have not filled more than a small part of the space
left by the secular decline of both old tradition and custom, as

might indeed be expected in societies in which the past becomes increasingly less relevant as a model or precedent for most forms of human behavior." Moreover, invented traditions, "are symptoms and therefore indicators of problems which might not otherwise be recognized, and developments which are otherwise difficult to identify and to date. They are evidence."[26] The same author reminds us that "tastes and fashions, notably in popular entertainment, can be 'created' only within very narrow limits; they have to be discovered before being exploited and shaped. It is the historian's business to discover them retrospectively—but also to try to understand why, in terms of changing societies in changing historical situations, such needs came to be felt."[27]

Responding to this issue, Alan Dundes points out the ambivalence on the part of intellectuals in matters that deal with the folk and folklore:

> [On the one hand,] the folk is a backward, illiterate segment of the population of which elitist intellectuals are ashamed. On the other hand, the folk represents the glorified, romanticized remnants of a national patrimony which is something for zealous intellectuals to celebrate. . . . The same situation applied in most countries. Intellectuals were both embarrassed by and proud of their folk and folklore. Inferiority breeds superiority![28]

For Dundes, the collection and study of folklore occurs generally in smaller countries (such as Finland, Hungary, and Ireland) that suffer from poor self-images in comparison with other nations. Countries that present a superiority complex (such as England and France) are not as interested in collecting or studying their own folklore. In the first type of country, we frequently find the phenomenon that Richard M. Dorson called *fakelore*, that is, "the presentation of spurious and synthetic writings under the claim that they are genuine folklore."[29]

The issue, however, does not focus on knowing whether a belief corresponds to some type of true reality but in analyzing why, even knowing such reality is contradicted by fact, there are groups that believe in it. Dundes examined what is considered to be one of the classic examples of *fakelore*, the Finnish epic poem *Kalevala*, published last century but presented by its inventor as having existed from time immemorial. Dundes points out that even though folklorists know this was an invented piece, the Finnish, including many intellectuals, preferred to believe it was an authentic folk epic: "The forces of romanticism and nationalism were—and are— so powerful in Finland that what the people *believe* was—and is— more important than what was true. So if the Finnish people believe the *Kalevala* is a folk epic, it does little good for Finnish (and foreign) folklorists to point out that the *Kalevala* is fakelore." Dundes continues his argument:

> Fakelore apparently fills a national, psychic need: namely, to assert one's national identity, especially in a time of crisis, and to instill pride in that identity. Hobsbawm claims that "Where the old ways are alive, traditions need be neither revived nor invented." It may be true that ideally folklore serves the cause of national identity cravings, but where folklore is deemed lacking or insufficient, individual creative writers imbued with national-istic zeal have felt free to fill in the void. They do so by creating a national epic or national "folk" hero *ex nihilo* if necessary, or what is more usual they embroider and inflate fragments of folk-lore into fakeloristic fabrications.[30]

When one analyzes the beliefs of social agents during these moments, it is common to point to a preoccupation surrounding the issue of a reality check. One of the frequent conclusions is that these beliefs are false. This conclusion places into debate the dif-ferent meanings of the word *truth*. Tzvetan Todorov argues for at least two different meanings of the term:

> The truth of correspondence and the truth of unveilment where the first term admits only all or nothing and the second term admits an approximation. The fact that X committed a crime is either true or false whatever the extenuating circumstances may be; the same is true in the knowledge that Jews either did or did not leave Auschwitz as smoke up the chimneys. However, if the issue is one of the causes of Nazism or of the identity of the aver-age Frenchman in 1987, neither answer of this type—yes or no— is conceivable: the answers can only approximate the truth more or less, since their goal is to unveil the nature of a phenomenon and not to establish facts. The novelist aspires only to the second type of truth; and he owes no lesson to the historian dealing with the first type of truth.[31]

Similarly, Dan Sperber makes a distinction between factual beliefs and representational beliefs. The former refer to "pure knowledge" whereas the latter are what we call "convictions," "persuasions," "opinions," "beliefs," and so on. When he analyzes apparently irrational beliefs, Sperber argues:

> A proposition can be paradoxical, counter-intuitive or self-contradictory, but in and by itself, it cannot be irrational. What can be rational or irrational is what one does with that proposition, for instance asserting it, denying it, entertaining it, using it as a premise in a logical derivation, etc. Thus to decide whether some belief is rational we need to know not only its content but also in which sense it is "believed."[32]

For these reasons, it is important to realize that all social groups, independent of their degree of economic development, have beliefs that when evaluated through evolutionary criteria will appear irrational. Comparing the beliefs of different groups, Paul Veyne questions:

> How is it possible to half-believe in contradictory things? Children believe that Santa Claus comes down the chimney, bringing them toys, and at the same time believe that these toys are put there by their parents. Do they then really believe in Santa Claus? Yes, and the faith of the Dorzé is no less whole. In the eyes of these Ethiopians, says Dan Sperber, the leopard is a Christian animal who respects the fast of the Coptic church, the observance of which, in Ethiopia, is the principal test of religion. Nonetheless, a Dorzé is no less careful to protect his livestock on Wednesdays and Fridays, the fast days, than on other days of the week. He holds it true that leopards fast and that they eat every day. Leopards are dangerous every day; this he knows by experience. They are Christians; tradition proves it.

To answer his own question, Veyne makes a comparison of the issue with the Greeks and their belief in their myths:

> Like the Dorzé, who imagine both that the leopard fasts and that one must be on guard against him every day, the Greeks believe and do not believe in their myths. They believe in them, but they use them and cease believing at the point where their interest in believing ends. It should be added in their defense that their bad faith resided in their belief rather than in their ulterior motives. Myth was nothing more than a superstition of the half-literate, which the learned called into question. The coexistence of con-

tradictory truths in the same mind is nonetheless a universal fact. Lévi-Strauss's sorcerer believes in his magic and cynically manipulates it. According to Bergson, the magician resorts to magic only when no sure technical recipes exist. The Greeks question the Pythia and know that sometimes this prophetess makes propaganda for Persia or Macedonia; the Romans fix their state religion for political purposes by throwing sacred fowl into the water if these do not furnish the necessary predictions; and all peoples give their oracles—or their statistical data—a nudge to confirm what they wish to believe. Heaven helps those who help themselves; Paradise, but the later the better. How could one not be tempted to speak of ideology here?[33]

This type of reflection is applied to the notion of myth that is frequently interpreted erroneously as the opposite of reality. This interpretation forgets that myth is an atemporal and all-encompassing narrative whose significant unity is preoccupied in resolving contradictions and issues that deal with the origin of natural phenomena.

Nevertheless, if myth is seen as a language characteristic of societies that have no historical time, this does not mean it has disappeared altogether in modern societies. In an analysis of everyday language in this type of society, Roland Barthes catalogues a widespread mythic presence. For Barthes, myth presents the unknown as deriving naturally from the known. In this way, the proper principle of myth is to transform history into nature and contingency into eternity. Myth does not propose to hide, but rather to deform. Whereby the specific function of myth is to transform meaning into form, myth is always a language robbery. Myth in modern societies is an apolitical speech that imagines itself eternal:

> Myth does not deny things, on the contrary, its function is to talk about them; simply, it purifies them, it makes them innocent, it gives them a natural and eternal justification, it gives them a clarity which is not that of an explanation but that of a statement of fact. . . . In passing from history to nature, myth acts economically: it abolishes the complexity of human acts, it gives them the simplicity of essences, it does away with dialects, with any going back beyond what is immediately visible, it organizes a world which is without contradictions because it is without depth, a world wide open and wallowing in the evident, it establishes a blissful clarity: things appear to mean something by themselves.[34]

We come to the question, then, of understanding the operations of these social constructions that we call representations, memory, identity, imaginary, and so on. All these processes involve an attribution of meaning to human actions, a discovery of differences, an appropriation and reelaboration of cultural manifestations, a resemantization, and so forth.

Nation and tradition are patches of reality; they are categories for the classification of people and space, and therefore they are forms of delineating borders and establishing limits. They function as basic points of reference around which identities are agglutinated. Identities are social constructions formulated through real or invented differences that operate as diacritical marks, that is, signs that confer a mark of distinction. In this sense, Lévi-Strauss affirms that identity is something abstract without any real existence, but it is indispensable as a point of reference.[35]

Although they may be abstract entities, identities—when seen as distinctive properties that differentiate and specify social groups—must be molded through everyday living. Thus, just as the relationship with parents during the first years of life determines the individual's own identity construction, so too the first cultural identities and experiences will be crucial for the construction of social identities, be these ethnic, religious, regional, or national.

Tolstoy is attributed with the saying that if a writer wants to be universal, this writer must begin by describing his village. This affirmation is significant for, although we are all universal in the sense that we belong to the human race, there exists an extensive series of mediations that go from the specific individual to the generic individual. In spite of the existence of a category we call "human being," humans come to be such in very specific and unique times, contexts, and circumstances.

The problematic of nation and tradition remains extremely current even in a world that is tending toward becoming a "global village." Some of the reasons for such timeliness are that people continue to be born in a determined country and region; they continue to speak the language, to acquire the customs, and to identify themselves with symbols and values that are particular to that nation or region; they continue to root for the national all-star team in the country's traditional sports; they continue to respect the flag and to be called on to defend their country's territorial boundaries and to die proudly for national honor.

Chapter Two

NATIONAL AND REGIONAL TRADITIONS IN THE CONSTRUCTION OF BRAZILIAN IDENTITY

●

The proclamation of the Brazilian Republic in 1889, sixty-seven years after Brazil's independence from Portugal, began a process of political and administrative decentralization that apparently went against the dominant contemporary tendency in Latin American and other countries where national identities and cross-regional alliances were being forged. However, as Barbara Weinstein indicates, if we examine those other countries, we can notice patterns of change that have much in common with the Brazilian process of decentralization, since, in general, the emergent bourgeoisie acquired control over certain state powers through alliances with rural elites in less developed regions. In some cases, when there existed geographical obstacles or merely partial transition toward a capitalist system of production, the emerging bourgeoisie that sought national power could, in reality, fortify the power of the traditional agrarian elites. Seen from this angle, the political history of the Old Republic would be much less atypical than it seems. We can therefore explain the strengthening of regionalism in Brazil during that period as "due mainly to the embryonic and uneven development of capitalist relations of production and the ongoing importance of export agriculture."[1]

Probably stemming from the social transformations that were taking place during the Old Republic,[2] one increasingly discerns the tendency to intellectualize the organization of society and state in Brazil, as well as to discuss questions of national and regional identity in the country. At that time—as it does today— the thinking of Brazilian intellectuals oscillated in these matters. Thus, in certain moments, Brazilian culture is extremely devalued by the elites who exchange it for European cultural models (or more recently North American). As a reaction, at other times, one notices that certain Brazilian cultural manifestations come to be valued to an extreme to the point of exalting certain national symbols.[3]

The first process is represented by a series of intellectuals like Sílvio Romero, Euclides da Cunha, Nina Rodrigues, Oliveira Vianna, and Arthur Ramos whose preoccupations with explaining Brazilian society through the interaction of race and environment make them extremely pessimistic and prejudiced when it comes to Brazilians. They tend to classify them, among other things, as apathetic and indolent, seeing their intellectual life as destitute in terms of philosophy and sciences and contaminated by a subjectivist and morbid lyricism.

The opposite process to that just explained is represented by the valorization of that which could be classified as more authentically Brazilian. This tendency is already present in the last century in the writings of the Indigenist school that reaches its apogee in the novels of José de Alencar who values Brazilian national roots: the Indian, rural life, and so on. The tendency to exalt the virtues of the Brazilian character continues in the twentieth century and remains a constant in the country's intellectual life.[4]

In 1922, when Brazil commemorated the centennial of its independence, in São Paulo the "Week of Modern Art" was celebrated. This event marked the beginning of the Modernist Movement that had as its goal the artistic and intellectual modernization of Brazil in relation to Europe. With all its ideological complexity and differentiation, the movement represents a dividing line in this panorama. On the one hand, it means the repositioning of Brazil in relation to the modern cultural and artistic movements occurring abroad; on the other hand, the movement also implies a search for national roots giving value to what was most autochthonous in Brazil.

One of the contributions of the movement consists precisely in having posed not only the question of the cultural-artistic modernizing of an underdeveloped society, but also the problematic of national identity. In this sense, beginning with the second phase of Modernism (from 1924 on), the attack toward the cult of the past is substituted by an emphasis on the elaboration of a national culture bringing about a rediscovery of Brazil by Brazilians. In spite of certain chauvinism and pride with respect to São Paulo, the Modernists refused the concept of regional identity, since they believed it was through a national identity that one would achieve a universal identity. Thus "for the Modernists, the process toward universal access goes through the affirmation of *brasilidade* [Brazilian national identity]."[5] This becomes clear in a letter from Mário de Andrade to Sérgio Milliet:

> Modern problem. The problem of being something. And one can only be, by being national. We have the modern, national, moralizing, human problem of Brazilianizing Brazil. Modern problem, modernism, take stock on the fact that today only national art is valued . . . And we will only become universal the day that the Brazilian coefficient enters the contest for a universal richness.[6]

A letter from Mário de Andrade to Carlos Drummond de Andrade points in the same direction: "We will only be civilized in relation to civilizations the day we create the ideal identity, the Brazilian orientation. Then we will advance from the mimetic toward the creation phase. And then we will be universal, because we will have become national."[7] Concordant with this attitude, Mário de Andrade became a self-named "apprentice tourist," developing an intense activity of research and trips to study those elements that comprise Brazilian culture.[8]

It is significant to note that the Modernist Movement of 1922 (the same year of the founding of the Brazilian Communist Party and of the first *tenentista*[9] revolt, as well as the centennial of Brazilian independence) appears in São Paulo, a city that is already claiming the status of a future industrial metropolis.[10] In 1926 the *Regionalist Manifesto* of Gilberto Freyre[11] was published in Recife, the

most developed capital in the Northeast. The 1926 Movement—
which fifty years later Freyre would call "regionalist, traditionalist,
and in its own way modernist"—is, in a certain way, the very opposite of that of 1922.[12] It is a movement that does not exalt innova-
tion which would modernize Brazilian culture in relation to that
present abroad, but one that, on the contrary, wishes to preserve
not only tradition in general, but particularly the traditions of an
economically less developed region.

The *Regionalist Manifesto* basically develops two interrelated
themes: the defense of the region as a unit of national organization
and the conservation of regional and traditional values in Brazil in
general and in the northeast region in particular.

An analysis of the document is extremely elucidating. It begins
affirming the existence, in Recife, of a movement to rehabilitate
regional and traditional values in the Northeast. Thus, every
Tuesday, an "apolitical group of regionalists meets for tea and traditional cakes and sweets from the region . . . prepared by the hands
of the mistresses of the house"[13] to discuss in a relaxed way the
problems of this part of Brazil.

It is interesting to observe that this is a meeting for men only.
The role reserved for women, who do not sit with the group, is the
subaltern role of servants who busy themselves with the feeding of
the intellectuals, men who consider themselves very important. In
spite of the "apolitical" and modest tone, Freyre is categorical with
respect to the goal of the group: "Our movement has as its objective nothing less than the inspiration of a new organization for
Brazil."[14] This proposal to reorganize the country with an eye
toward consolidating Brazilian society is formulated through a
political, administrative model rooted in the region as the essential
element in the concept of nation, for it is the set of regions and not
an arbitrary collection of states that would truly form Brazil. Since,
from its beginning, the country was made up of natural regions
onto which social regions were mapped, it must be administered
regionally.

The necessity of reorganizing Brazil—the first central theme of
the *Manifesto* and a constant preoccupation for the thinkers of the
end of the last century and beginning of this one—would stem from
the fact that Brazil suffers, since it is a nation-state, from the evil
consequences of foreign models that are imposed on it without consideration of its peculiarities and geographical and social diversity.

As can be seen, the formulation of an alternative system of organization for Brazil is anchored in the indictment of the practice of
importing foreign models considered incompatible with the country's peculiarities. The debate about whether to import foreign
models and ideas is a recurring theme among Brazilian intellectuals and is treated in the 1926 *Manifesto* in the analysis of the question of tradition.

When he emphasized the need for a cross-regional articulation,
Freyre touched on an important and modern point, that is, how to
enable regional differences to survive within a national unity in a
country as extensive as Brazil. This type of preoccupation also
appears in works published subsequently to the *Manifesto*. In a
1944 lecture in the United States, suggestively titled, "Unity and
Diversity, Nation and Region," Freyre affirms this notion:

> A region may be politically less than a nation. But vitally and cul-
> turally it is more than a nation; it is more basic both as a condi-
> tion of life and as a medium of expression or creativeness. To be
> a genuine philosopher a man has to be super- or supranational;
> but he can hardly be supraregional in the sense of ignoring the
> regional condition of the life, the experience, the culture, the art,
> and the thought that he is considering or analyzing.[15]

This is precisely the conclusion that the Modernists reached
after the second phase of the movement when they realized that
the only way to have a universal identity was to have a national
identity first. Taking into consideration the differences in relation
to the Modernists, what Freyre is affirming is that the only way to
have a national identity, in a country like Brazil, is to have a
regional identity first.

However, in a way, his logic is the inverse of that of the
Modernists, since it is not rooted in a cultural modernization
through foreign modern values, but, on the contrary, it is rooted in
the criticism toward the evils of progress and the importation of
foreign customs and values. Thus, for example, when he analyzes
the Northeast, he affirms that this region is in the process of losing
the consciousness of its historical values and of its possibilities
because of the process of standardization that comes from world
industrialization and the effects of similar influences in Brazil:

> The danger of cultural monotony or excessive unification of cul-
> ture within that American continent sprang from the influence

of North American capitalistic industrialism, largely dominated by the idea that what is good for North Americans should be good for every other people of America.[16]

For those who accompanied the heated debates about the future of Brazil during the populist phase (1945–1964), the end of this quote will immediately bring to mind the criticism toward politicians who affirmed that "what is good for the United States is good for Brazil." Of course, Freyre's perspective and that of the populists are quite different. The former could be labeled "conservative," and the latter "progressive" as they frequently called themselves. However, both perspectives have in common a criticism toward foreign influences on the country and on Brazilian culture.

The conservation of regional and traditional values in Brazil in general and in the Northeast in particular is the second great theme in the *Regionalist Manifesto*. Freyre begins by speaking in defense of northeast values and traditions:

Of the danger of their being altogether abandoned, such is the neophyte furor of those in power who, among us, pretend to be advanced and progressive because they blindly imitate foreign fashions. Foreign fashion in general. In particular, that fashion in the states or in provinces that Rio or São Paulo believe to be "elegant" and "modern": including that carnivalesque Santa Claus who, with his winter boots designed for snow, crushes the old Brazilian, green, sweet-smelling, summertime nativity scenes. He is lending a ridiculous note to our family Christmases that are now adorned with foreign trees brought from Europe or from the United States by the bourgeois characterized by pretentiousness and money.[17]

This is a criticism levied against Brazilian elites who had the habit of adopting customs they judged to be modern. This tendency was already described by Maria Isaura Pereira de Queiroz with respect to the city of Rio de Janeiro on the occasion of the coming of the Portuguese royal family at the beginning of the nineteenth century.[18] This criticism is also somewhat reminiscent of the notion of "out-of-place ideas" described by Roberto Schwarz in relation to the adoption of foreign ideologies that were then reelaborated to fit local needs.[19]

It is significant that Freyre chooses items pertaining to what is considered backward or symbols of poverty or both when he proposes his strong defense of northeastern values and the need to preserve them. Thus, for example, he weaves a praise of the *mocambo* (a natural shelter made of existing plants in the brush and trees, primarily in the Northeast) as an illustration of the northeastern contribution to Brazilian culture, in the sense that it is a human shelter adapted from the tropical environment and is an economic solution to the problem of a poverty-stricken home: "the maximum use, by man, of the regional environment, represented by wood, straw, vines, grass, all easy and reachable by the poor."[20]

The text also defends the narrow streets and criticizes the tendency, then beginning, of constructing great avenues and changing regional names of streets and old places (like Sun Street, Fried Fish Alley, Loneliness Street) to the names of those who are powerful at the moment or to politically insignificant dates.

Another aspect defended by Freyre is northeastern culinary art. After affirming that northeastern culinary tradition in its totality is in crisis and that canned and pickled candy are fashionable, Freyre predicts the following:

> A culinary in crisis means that an entire civilization is in danger: the danger of losing its characteristics and personality. The new generations of young ladies no longer know, among us, except among the more modest groups, how to make a dessert or a traditional or regional dish. They no longer want to or have the time to read old family cookbooks when the truth is that, after religious books pertaining to Mass, dessert and traditional dish cookbooks are those that must receive women's most attentive reading. A sense of devotion and obligation must complement each other in Brazilian women, turning them into good Christians, and at the same time good cooks so they may be better mothers and contribute to the national happiness. A people cannot be happy when women lack culinary art. It is almost as serious a lack as that of religious faith.[21]

Again, women had the role of feeding. Thus the recipe books would help to form good mothers—the most important contribution that Freyre attributes to women in the process of constructing a national Brazilian identity. Placing himself as the bastion for the defense of the popular that must be protected from "evil cosmopolitanism and false modernism,"[22] the author of the *Manifesto* builds an opposition that, in the final analysis, can be summarized as follows: popular and regional are equivalent to traditional (and good), whereas cosmopolitanism is equivalent to modernism (and bad). His position is similar to the vision of the Romantics who occupied themselves with popular culture in Europe in the nineteenth century and for whom the authenticity contained in popular manifestations constituted the essence of national identity. From this perspective, the common people are seen as "a homogeneous and autonomous whole, whose spontaneous creativity represented the highest expression of human values and the way of life to which humanity should return."[23]

This becomes clear, for example, when Freyre affirms the following:

> In the Northeast, those who get close to the common folk reach the roots and the source of life, culture, and regional art. Those who approach the common people are among masters and become apprentices no matter what art degrees they have or what doctor's degrees in medicine. The force of Joaquim Nabuco, of Sílvio Romero, of José de Alencar . . . , of other great northeastern expressions of culture and of Brazilian spirit, came primarily from the contact they had when children in the sugar mills or in the city, or after they become adults, the contact with the common folks.[24]

The comparison with nineteenth-century European Romantics is enlightening. Analyzing their position in Germany of that century, Renato Ortiz demonstrated how at the time the problematic of national identity was a central question since the German nation did not exist as a political and cultural unity. "It is from this context that the debate about popular culture springs; part of the German intelligentsia turns its attention to popular traditions and through them tries to legitimize a culture that is authentically national."[25]

The same author states that "while modernism is linked to the advancement and consolidation of an urban middle class, Gilberto Freyre represents the dimension of an aristocratic, rural power that sees itself threatened. The conflict can be clearly described as a struggle between intellectuals from one social order that is being overtaken by history and the organic intellectuals of a new type of society that is being constructed."[26]

Focusing merely on the conservative character of the *Manifesto*, however, does not exhaust its meaning. In truth, a rereading of it, after more than seventy years from the date of its publication, is impressive for the modernity of the themes studied. One's attention is drawn to the fact that a document elaborated in the 1920s deals with questions that, at the end of the century, continue to be important and are far from being resolved.

It could be argued that at least two distinct readings of the *Regionalist Manifesto* are possible. The first would find in it a document elaborated by an intellectual who represents a rural aristocracy and who sees the established social order going through transformations that place the traditional pattern of domination in check. His reaction reflects a traditionalist point of view; it is similar to the aristocratic reactions that were prevalent before the changes urbanization and industrialization brought about and that were based on a criticism of the loss of community values and cultural purity that supposedly had existed in the past.

In this line of interpretation, one could see in the defense of the region a strategy of someone who sees northeastern oligarchies increasingly lose power and who tries to place the union of regional peripheries in opposition to a central power. Similarly, one could see in the intransigent defense of popular traditions and values a wistful position that tries to erect a crystallized popular culture in a symbol of national identity to be juxtaposed to a modernity defined as foreign.

Without setting any of these arguments aside, a second reading would point, however, to the fact that behind the conservative orientation of the *Manifesto* are themes that continue to be very modern in Brazil. It is precisely in the fusion of a conservative perspective with the raising of questions not yet resolved in Brazil that the *Regionalist Manifesto* is original. In fact, the *Manifesto* brings to light a series of questions that are recurrent in Brazilian history: union versus federation, nation versus region, unity versus diversity, national versus foreign, popular versus erudite, tradition versus modernity.

Brazilians continue to argue the formulation of models to organize the nation, and this debate inevitably comes to the discussion of what is national (and therefore authentic for some but somewhat less developed for others) and what is foreign (and therefore spurious for some but modern for others); that is, Brazilians continue to revolve around the question of national identity. This question is posed again and made part of the current debate as new contexts are created.

If the Old Republic was characterized by political and administrative decentralization, the New Republic, which started in 1930, reverts this tendency and accentuates a growing centralization in the most disparate levels. This process needs to be understood as the passage of important transformations that had been in gestation in the first decades of the twentieth century and that assumed a greater dimension during the 1930s and afterward. In other words, these changes came about through the formation of a nondurable goods import substitution industry, through the growth of cities that became centers for regional markets, through the coffee crisis, through the failure of the system based on political combinations among the rural oligarchies (the "governors' policy"), and through the appearance of social and military revolts that began in the 1920s and culminated with the 1930 Revolution.[27] These processes taking place during the Old Republic and the consequences of the world crisis of 1929 set in motion changes that fundamentally affected the country.

It is from this period that the apparatus of a more centralized state is created and that power moves more and more from a regional to a national arena. From the economic point of view, for example, the central government abolishes interstate taxes and begins to intervene more in the economy, helping to bring about the use of surpluses created by the rural oligarchies toward the initiation of a new process of industrialization, albeit maintaining the privileges of these oligarchies in a modified way. At the social level, the state regulates the relationships between capital and work, creating a labor legislation and a Ministry of Labor. A Ministry of Education is also created, which plays a fundamental role in the development of national identity by disseminating a national education standard. Thus the culture of ethnic minorities, frequently the standard in the regions, had their influence weakened.[28]

During this period, ideologies surrounding the Brazilian national character that emphasized the difficulty of building a true culture in Brazil because of racial miscegenation give way to positions like that of Gilberto Freyre which underscore the idea that a racial democracy existed in Brazil.

From this time on, one had to rethink a country that had experimented with a process of political and economic consolidation and that had to face the consequences of the 1929 crisis and of World War II. Nationalism gained impetus and the state stabilized. In fact, it was the state that took on the task of building the nation. This tendency was further accentuated with the implantation of the *Estado Novo* [New State][29] when the elected governors were substituted by intervenors and the states' militias lost strength—measures that increased administrative and political centralization. At the cultural and ideological level, the prohibition of the teaching of foreign languages, the introduction of a class in Morality and Civics, the creation of the Department of Press and Propaganda (which had as its mission, besides censorship, the exaltation of the work ethic) helped to create a model of national identity that was centralized.

It was significant that the constitution decreed by Getúlio Vargas on 10 November 1937 initiating the *Estado Novo* suppressed state flags by affirming in Article 2 that "the use of the national flag, the national anthem, and the national coat of arms is obligatory throughout the country. There will be no other flags, anthems, nor coats of arms. The law will regulate the use of national symbols."[30]

Less than a month after the implantation of the New State, Vargas ordered the ceremony of the burning of state flags. The event took place along the Russell Esplanade in Rio de Janeiro commemorating simultaneously Flag Day (a celebration that had been postponed) and the honoring of the victims of the Intentona Comunista[31] [Communist uprising] of 1935. In this ritual, which symbolized a greater unification of the country and a weakening of regional and state powers, twenty-one Brazilian flags were raised in place of the twenty-one state flags burned in a large bonfire in the middle of the plaza to the sound of the national anthem played by several bands and sung by thousands of schoolchildren under the direction of Heitor Villa Lobos, famous Brazilian composer. After the burning of the flags, Minister of Justice Francisco Campos delivered this address:

> Brazilian Flag, today you are the only one. You are being raised today throughout the national territory, the one and only, there being no place in the hearts of Brazilians for any other pennant, flag, or symbol. Brazilians united themselves around Brazil and decreed with determination that this time they will not consent

to the divisiveness of discord, that Brazil is the one and only fatherland and that there is no place for any other ideology in Brazil, nor is there space and devotion for any flag other than this one, today being raised with the blessings of the Church, the salute of the swords, the veneration of the people, and the songs of the youth. You are the only one because there is only one Brazil—re-creating around you once again the unity of Brazil, the unity of thought and action, the unity that is conquered by the will and by the heart, the unity that can only reign when it is established through historical decisions coming among public discord and enmity, a single moral and political order, a sovereign order, brought about by strength and ideals, the order of a single ideology and of a single authority, the ideology and authority of Brazil.[32]

To be sure, the modifications that occurred from 1930 to 1945 are profound. Thus when at the end of World War II the New State ends and a National Constitutional Assembly is elected to think through a new model of administrative and political organization, Brazil has become a different country. Brazilians had begun to discard their rural vocations, and manufacturing was becoming responsible for 20 percent of the gross national product. The construction of roads and the abolition of the states' autonomy helped to unify internal markets as well as to diminish the power of local oligarchies. The migration from the country to the city was accentuated and created a new protagonist in the political scene: the urban masses that would be considered as social agents by populism.

The problem of national versus foreign and a federation of states versus central government has been a constant in Brazilian politics. Thus after the war, more specifically from 1946 to 1964, the national identity question is once again debated heatedly by many, the ISEB (*Instituto Superior de Estudos Brasileiros*) and the CPC (*Centro Popular de Cultura*)[33] being eloquent examples. At the time, one of the accusations directed toward Brazilian intellectuals was that they would be colonized and that they would contribute to the creation of an alienated culture as a result of a dependency status; hence the necessity of a vanguard to help produce an authentic national culture for the people, a vague and polyclassist category.

The themes of progress and modernity were also hot during this period. It was a matter of overcoming the condition of underdevelopment in a battle that featured industry as a key element. Import substitution industries evolved, this time dealing with durable goods, thus creating an even greater dependence on foreign capital. At the same time organizations such as the SUDENE (*Superintendência do Desenvolvimento do Nordeste*)[34] arose, with the specific mission of reducing regional inequalities such as that which existed in the Northeast.

The transfer of the capital from Rio de Janeiro to Brasília in 1960 would propitiate a march to the West and consequent territorial integration, bringing about heated debates over the necessity of spending so much money toward this end and over the new capital's daring architecture which was considered extremely modern and advanced.

In 1964 the military took over power and initiated a process of conservative modernization. A growing political, economic, and administrative centralization occurred through the integration of the national market; through the implantation of networks of roads, telephones, and mass communication; through the concentration of taxes at the federal level; through the control of states' military forces by the army; and through intervention in state politics. All these processes diminished state powers substantially so that if we compare the position of state presidents during the Old Republic to that of governors elected indirectly after 1964 we will see that the latter, as a rule, were nothing more than hand-picked by the president of the Republic in a situation similar to that of the intervenors of the New State, whereas the former enjoyed considerable autonomy.[35]

The new regime carried the accumulation of capital to higher thresholds. This was done in association with foreign capital. There was a new process of import substitutions, so that at this time almost all consumer goods were produced within the national borders, and many of these goods were even exported. Among them were goods of a symbolic nature, such as soap operas.

A new situation, from the economic, political, and cultural points of view, is being configured. The Tropicalist Movement begun in 1968 was characterized by the appearance of new composers of popular music who used both rhythm and lyrics to show the contrast between the traditional and the modern in Brazil, thus reappropriating the preoccupations of the Modernist Movement of 1922. The Tropicalist Movement posited within a symbolic realm that

Brazilian reality had changed considerably. In fact, Brazil had undergone a process of unequal and combined development, creating a picture showing extreme misery on the one hand and elements of technological progress and modernity on the other. It is significant that the creators of Tropicalism were artists from the Northeast, the region that continued in its process of marginalization.

During this period the debate about national and regional identity continues, but it is discussed in new terms. Once again the central state takes on the role of being the creator and bastion of national identity. The central government is responsible for promoting progress while at the same time keeping alive the national collective memory. That this same central government was responsible for bringing about an intense denationalization in the economy was not seen as contradictory since these two questions—identity and economy—are taken as two separate issues. It is significant, in this sense, that it is precisely the multinationals, such as Shell and Xerox, that carry out the defense of Brazilian folklore in their publications.

With the battle for redemocratization of the country and with the process of political opening that marked the end of the military cycle, old questions began to resurface. Thus in spite of—or perhaps because of—the growing centralization, today one observes tendencies contrary to it. These tendencies are manifested by an emphasis on the need for a true federalism, on the proclamation of the advantages of an administrative decentralization, on the clamor for a tributary reform that may deliver more resources to the states and municipalities, and on the affirmation of regional and state identities that emphasize differences compared to the rest of Brazil.

The affirmation of regional identities in Brazil may be seen as a reaction to cultural homogeneity and as way of making salient those cultural differences. This rediscovery of differences and the modernity of the issue of a federation at a time when the country finds itself quite integrated from the political, economic, and cultural points of view suggest that, in Brazil, what is national is first of all regional.

CARACAS

VENEZUELA

COLOMBIA
●BOGOTÁ

GEORGETOWN

GUYNA
PARAMABIRO

SURINAME ● CAYENNE
FRENCH GUIANA (Fr)

RORAIMA

ATLANTIC

OCEAN   EQUATOR

QUITO
●
EQUADOR

AMAPÁ

AMAZONAS

PARÁ

MARANHÃO

CEARÁ RIO
       GRANDE
       DO NORTE

PERU

ACRE

RONDÔNIA

PIAUI

PARAIBA

PERNAMBUCO

ALAGOAS
SERGIPE

MATO
GROSSO

TOCANTINS

BRASILIA

BAHIA

●LIMA

●LA PAZ

GOIÁS

BOLIVIA

MATO
GROSSO
DO SUL

MINAS
GERAIS

ESPIRITO
SANTO

SÃO
PAOLO

RIO DE JANEIRO

TROPIC OF
CAPRICORN

PARAGUAY
ASUNCION

PARANÁ

PACIFIC

OCEAN

SANTA
CATARINA

RIO
GRANDE
DO
SUL

PORTO
ALEGE

ARGENTINA

SANTIAGO
●
CHILE

URUGUAY

●MONTEVIDÉO

BUENOS AIRES

LEGEND

——— International boundary

----- State boundary

☐ Federal district

○ State capital

• National capital

SCALE
1:5,000,000

Chapter Three

RIO GRANDE DO SUL AND
BRAZIL: A CONTRADICTORY
RELATIONSHIP

●

The state of Rio Grande do Sul is generally seen as occupying a unique position in relation to Brazil. This perception is the result of its geographical characteristics, its strategic position, the form in which it was populated, its economy, and the way in which it has been part of the national history. In spite of the state's having great internal heterogeneity (from the point of view of geography, ethnicity, economics, and colonization), it is frequently juxtaposed to the rest of the country as a whole. The uniqueness of the relationship between the state and the nation has prompted other Brazilians to refer jokingly to the state as "that neighboring and sister country in the South."

Historically, a recurring theme in the relationship between the state of Rio Grande do Sul and Brazil is precisely the tension between autonomy and integration. The emphasis on the state's peculiarities and the simultaneous affirmation of its belonging to Brazil constitutes one of the primary foundations for the social construction of the *Gaúcho* identity. This identity is constantly brought up to date, restated, and evoked.

First, there is the so-called geographical isolation of the state of

Rio Grande do Sul that is responsible for the state's being "an entity separated from the rest of the world by its coastal sandy areas, by its rivers, by its mountains, and by its forests."[1] Nature, while prizing Rio Grandians with one of the most favorable physical spaces for human activity and well-being, provided them, at the same time, with a position of difficult access. Nature isolated people in the Rio Grandian Continent[2] and thereby caused their isolation from the rest of Brazil for some two centuries.

We must add to this geographical peculiarity a history that can only be characterized as sui generis. This history begins with a late integration into the rest of the country. Thus, although discovered at the beginning of the fifteenth century, it is not until more than a century later that Rio Grande do Sul begins to participate in economic activities of colonial Brazil through the preying of wild cattle with the primary objective of exporting leather to Europe through Buenos Aires or Sacramento. It is as recently as the end of the seventeenth century that these cattle gained importance on the national level when they began to have an internal market in the budding mining industry in the zone of the Gerais. The new industry stimulated people from São Paulo and Laguna to come herd the wild cattle in Rio Grande do Sul and take the cattle to the mining area.

The objective of the Portuguese crown was, however, to populate the land from the south of São Vicente to the Colony of Sacramento (founded by this same Crown in 1680) and, in this sense, Rio Grande do Sul carried out "a strategic function as a point of support for the conservation of the Portuguese holdings in the Prata region."[3] This function prompted the Crown, at the beginning of the eighteenth century, to distribute land grants [Sesmarias][4] to the cattle traders so they might settle on the land as well as to the military so they might create cattle ranches. The military conflicts surrounding the Sacramento Colony and the border disputes meant a growing militarization of the region, that, in 1760, became a captaincy with the name of Rio Grande de São Pedro Captaincy.

The strategic position of Rio Grande do Sul gives it the image of a frontier: located at the edge of Brazil, it could belong to Brazil or to other countries depending on the results of the historical forces at play. Responding to a northeastern writer who considered the Gaúcho to be more Spanish and belonging more to the Prata region than to the Brazilian region, the novelist Erico Veríssimo defined this situation of threshold:

> We are a frontier. In the eighteenth century, when the Portuguese and Spanish soldiers fought for the definitive occupation of this then immense desert, we had to make a choice: remain with the Portuguese or with the Spanish. We paid a heavy tribute of suffering and blood to remain on this side of the southernmost border of Brazil. How can you accuse us of Spanishlike behavior? We have been, from colonial times until the end of the century, a chronically incendiary territory. In seventy-seven years we have had twelve armed conflicts, counting the revolutions. We lived in permanent readiness for war. Rarely were our women not in mourning. Think about the harsh activities of country life—herding, domesticating, and branding the wild horses, herding the animals, leaving for the daily routine the need to break the heavy frost during winter daybreaks—and you will understand why virility became the most sought after and appreciated quality of the Gaúcho. This type of life is responsible for the somewhat impetuous tendencies that remained in the collective unconscious of these populations, and it explains our roughness, our disconcerting frankness, at times, our habit of speaking loudly, as if shouting orders, often giving others the impression that we live in a permanent state of horsemanship. The truth is, however, that none of the authentic heroes of Rio Grande I met ever pontificated, ever bragged about any act of braveness. My fellow Rio Grandians who after the victory in the 1930 revolution set out for Rio [de Janeiro] in costume and tied their horses to the obelisk at Rio Branco Avenue—those were not legitimate Gaúcho, they were parodies like those in the operetta genre.[5]

In this quote, Erico Veríssimo evokes elements that are recurring in the Gaúcho discourse. The first is the frontierlike character of the state. The second is the choice the state made: Rio Grande preferred to belong to Brazil when it could have opted to belong to the Spanish Empire. The third is the high price that was paid for this option represented by the wars involving the state and by the need the state felt to bring about insurrection against the central government when it perceived itself a victim of injustice—a need to intervene in national politics in moments of crisis. The fourth element is the existence of a specific social type—the Gaúcho—marked by virility and courage when facing an enemy and when required to fight the forces of nature and face arduous frontier life. The fifth element touches the question of authenticity of customs and behavior. Also noticeable here is the presence of women who always appear in mourning. They appear in this text in an indirect form as a consequence of men's belligerent actions. But it is frequently up to them, in their condition of being orphans, widows, and mothers who lost their sons, to assume the responsibility of caring for the family. Women create (give birth) whereas men destroy (kill).

What one gleans from this set of elements is a constant climate of adversity. The necessity of guaranteeing the border, of dominating nature, of rebelling against the transgressions of the central government, besides fighting the state's own internal conflicts, helps to explain the somewhat impetuous character that has been incorporated into the Gaúcho collective unconscious.

The peculiarities of Rio Grande do Sul contribute to the construction of a series of representations surrounding the state that end up acquiring an almost mythic force which projects these images even today and allows them to contribute to actions and dictate current practices.

In spite of the internal diversity of the state (to the point that one author speaks of the "twelve Rio Grandes"[6]), regional tradition and historiography tend to represent its inhabitants through a single social type—the Gaúcho, the horseman and farmhand in the southwestern region of Rio Grande do Sul. Although he is Brazilian, he would be very different from other social types in the nation, having more proximity at times with his homonymic counterpart in Argentina or Uruguay. In the social construction of the Brazilian Gaúcho identity, there is a constant reference to elements that evoke a glorious past into which his figure was forged. His existence was marked by life in the wide open spaces, by the presence of a horse, by the border status with the Prata region, by his virility and the courage he expresses whether facing an enemy or the forces of nature, by his loyalty, by his honor, and so on.

But the figure of the Gaúcho, such as we know it, has gone through a long process of cultural elaboration before it achieved the current gentrified meaning of a citizen of the state of Rio Grande do Sul. Tracing the history of the word *Gaúcho*, August Meyer demonstrated that it did not always have the heroic meaning it acquired in regional literature and historiography. During the colonial period, the inhabitant of Rio Grande was called *guasca*[7] and later *gaudério* (vagrant, vagabond). This latter term had a pejorative sense and referred to the adventurers from São Paulo who deserted the regular troops and adopted the rough life of the leather traders and cattle thieves. They were errant vagabonds and thieves of contraband cattle in a region where the border was quite movable because of the conflicts between Portugal and Spain. At the end of the eighteenth century, they were called *Gaúchos*, a term that will keep the same pejorative connotations until early in the nineteenth century when, with the organization of the large ranches, it comes to mean peon and warrior in an encomiastic sense.[8]

What occurred was a re-semantization of the term, through which a social type previously considered deviant and marginalized was appropriated, reelaborated, and acquired a new positive meaning to the point of being transformed into a symbol of regional identity.[9] Flávio Loureiro Chaves argues the following:

> As he was disfigured and distanced from his origins, the Gaúcho was also made noble. What made him noble was this gentrified perspective of the great rural property owners who were directly interested in establishing an identity for him between the peon and the soldier, attributing to the Gaúcho a heroic aura. What made him noble later was the word of historians who made him a protagonist in a Brazilian epic that goes from the Prata region wars to the Paraguay Campaign, passing through the Farroupilha Revolution of 1835. The process of constructing the Gaúcho as a cattleman and warrior represents essentially an ideological phenomenon that placed him within a historical space where the attributes of courage, virility, subtlety, and mobility are demanded at all times, transferring him to the mythical plane. And there is no case in which the victory of ideology is so clearly transparent.[10]

The representations of the Gaúcho, which are now considered common knowledge, can be seen in the accounts of foreign travelers like Auguste Saint-Hilaire and Arsène Isabelle. These images are also present in a vast literary tradition that has as its origin the book *O Gaúcho*, published in 1870 during the height of Romanticism, and written by José de Alencar, an author who idealizes and mythifies the Gaúcho, calling him the "centaur of the pampas,"[11] never having even visited Rio Grande do Sul.

From a sociological perspective, Oliveira Vianna, a thinker from the state of Rio de Janeiro, in his classic *Southern Populations of Brazil*, on analyzing the Rio Grandian cattleman, attributed to him special characteristics and a specific mentality that distinguished him from the social types of the northeastern backlands and of the forests in the south-central part of the country. The differences in relation to other social types were caused by the environment and by the political superiority that derived from the Gaúcho's war experience: "The Gaúcho is socially a product of the pampas, as he is politically a product of war." Thus war experience gave to the Gaúcho elite *"the capacity for the command of large human masses and the practice of organizing them,"* at the same time that such war experience "developed in the collective conscience of those people, aside from the interdependence between social life and private family life . . . also the feeling and the *value of government as the supreme organ for collective interests."*

The cited author is also the most well-developed theoretician of the so-called southern democracy, when he argues that in Rio Grande do Sul there was a *"tradition of equality and familiarity between bosses and servants,* this interpenetrating of the two rural classes—the high and the low, the master and the servant—a phenomenon that constitutes, in its substance, the spirit of the Rio Grandian democracy." A decisive element for the creation of the social democracy would be the environment, responsible for the lightness of the work: "The pampas—with its amplitude, its freedom, its vast horizons, its grassy vegetation—makes a veritable sport out of the pastoral work."[12]

The idea of a social democracy was added to that of a racial democracy based on a classic quote by Saint-Hilarie, when the wise Frenchman affirmed the following:

> There is not, I believe, in all Brazil, a place where slaves are happier than in this captaincy. The masters work as much as the slaves, keeping themselves near and treating them with less scorn. The slave eats as he wishes; he is not poorly dressed; he does not travel on foot, and his principal occupation consists in galloping through the fields, something that is more healthy than tiring. Furthermore, they provide the animals around them with a superiority that consoles them about their low conditions, elevating themselves in their own eyes.[13]

In another part of his book, however, Saint-Hilarie makes this assertion more relative: "I affirmed that in this captaincy the blacks were treated with kindness and the whites were much more familiar with them than in other parts of the country. I was referring to the slaves in the ranches, a small number; in the beef jerky processing plants the picture changes, because since blacks are great in number and filled with vices brought from the capital, it becomes necessary to treat them with more energy."[14]

The argument that in Rio Grande do Sul the life of the slaves was easier when compared to that in other places rests on a confusion between the slaves from the ranches (a slave who was present in the state from its colonization, not belonging, however, to the productive process) and the slaves of the meat-processing plants. This misunderstanding brought about an "idealized" vision of the living conditions of blacks in the state. Examining the ideology of "racial democracy" and of "Gaúcho rural democracy," Fernando Henrique Cardoso argued that "as an ideology, besides not corresponding to the real conditions of social existence, it is formally contradictory in itself: it supposes a relationship between masters, slaves, indentured servants, peons that is at the same time autocratic and democratic, gentrified and egalitarian."[15]

Although there were black slaves in Rio Grande do Sul from the first half of the eighteenth century, their importance is accentuated from the end of that century, in activities such as wheat production, cattle farming, and primarily meat processing. In this latter activity, the work was entirely based on the figure of the slave. If the slaves' living conditions on the farms were considered good by several foreign travelers, the meat-processing plants were characterized by extreme inhumanity, attested to in several accounts.

In 1814, 29 percent of the population of Rio Grande do Sul was made up of slaves, and in 1862 this percentage was 27.3 percent. In the words of Cardoso, "If it is true that, together, the proportion of blacks and slaves was not the majority in Rio Grande, except in one or another town in the area of the old settlement, the number of captive blacks was always considerable, and the economic activity depended to a great extent on the work of the regular slave."[16]

Blacks also played an important role in the Farroupilha Revolution, and they comprised, according to the calculations of the Imperial Army, one-third to one-half of the rebel army.[17]

Margaret Marchiori Bakos points out that "it is commonplace in the historiography of Rio Grande do Sul to attribute to the rebels the ideals of black abolitionist movements. The idea is normally affirmed by citing Paragraph 4 of the Peace Treaty of Poncho Verde which states: 'Free and recognized as such are all the captive people who fought on the side of the Republic.'" However, Bento Gonçalves, the main leader of the Farroupilha Revolution, "at the same time that he requests, as a condition of peace, that the slaves who were at the service of the Republic be liberated by the imperial government, he leaves as an inheritance upon his death, in 1847, fifty-three slaves on his Camaquã farm. Others who belonged to the revolutionary movement also owned slaves several years after the end of the armed struggle."[18]

The presence of the Indian is also extremely faint in the social construction of Rio Grande do Sul's identity. Traditional historiography commonly refers to the Rio Grandian territory at the beginning of the Iberian colonization as "no-man's-land." In this operation, indigenous populations were not considered since they were seen as "faithless, kingless, and lawless." Archaeological research demonstrates, however, that Rio Grande do Sul was already populated more than twelve thousand years ago.

In the seventeenth century, the *bandeirantes*[19] [flag bearers] came in pursuit of Indians, some of whom were living in Jesuit reductions. The founding by the Jesuits of the Seven Peoples of the Missions around 1682 resulted in the creation of economic centers of great importance where the Indians raised cattle and planted *mate* tea (bitter tea served in gourds, which Gaúchos drink through a silver straw). Perceived as a "Theocratic Empire in America," the Seven Peoples began to preoccupy Portugal and Spain and, in 1750, became a pawn in the Treaty of Madrid, which ascertained that Portugal would turn over Sacramento to Spain and would keep the Missions. This action motivated the "Guarani Guerrilla" (1754–56), which was instigated by Indians led by Sepé Tiaraju. These Indians were not willing to turn over their lands.

It is estimated that today some nine thousand Indians live in Rio Grande do Sul, comprising 0.1 percent of the state's total population—the same proportion of all Brazilian Indians in relation to the Brazilian population. This is an indication of the systematic elimination of Indians from Rio Grande do Sul, which accounts for the small number existing there today. This purge was brought about by the white man's predatory contact with the Indians, characterized by death through wars, epidemics, and land appropriation, in a process similar to that occurring in the rest of the country. The massacres conducted by the São Paulo *bandeirantes* who came to enslave the Indians and the destruction of the Guarani Missions all contributed to this outcome. Surely a certain degree of miscegenation existed between whites and Indians and between blacks and Indians, which has been pointed out by various authors,[20] but we have no specific data to attest to that.

Just as traditional state historiography underestimates the presence of blacks, it also distances the Indian from the formation of the Gaúcho identity, contrary to what happened in the rest of Brazil after the 1930s. Thus Moysés Vellinho, a very respected historian, writing in the 1950s about the formation of Rio Grande do Sul, makes a distinction between the Gaúcho from the Prata region and the one from Rio Grande. Whereas the former were marked by miscegenation of Spaniards with Indian women, creating the mixed breed, an angry type that explains the origin of the dictator (*caudilho*), in Brazil nothing of the sort occurred. Thus "in the anthropological formation of our cowboy, the Indian not only entered with a much poorer contingent, but he brought a soul that lacked the hate with which he had reacted to the Spaniards' scorn and ferocity in the Prata region campaigns." Thus "one cannot escape the conclusion that, as a factor of historical integration, the Indian was of a mediocre significance among us." Speaking about the Missions, the same author states:

> The human material experimented with there was of the lowest substance, almost not usable, if not totally unusable as a factor in civilization. The Jesuits themselves were convinced of this, although so often they stated the opposite in documents written for the public. It would be difficult, in fact, to construct anything stable and lasting with the Indian as a foundation. They are an impoverished people who perhaps should not even be considered as a standard for a primitive race, but one that is in a state of true regression. We know that their intelligence, under the education of the priests, evolved satisfactorily up to their twelfth birthday. At this point, their intellectual growth stopped or began a process of involution.[21]

It is significant that a contemporary author, who proposes to revise history, wrote an article during the 1980s with the suggestive title "The Miscegenation That Never Occurred," in which, after criticizing authors like Vellinho and without adding any new data, he comes to the following conclusion:

> What happened was a total physical extinction of the Indian in Rio Grande do Sul as a result of a process of more than three centuries during which the following occurred: (a) a deadly war of the white man against the Indian; (b) an occupation of all Indian lands by the colonizer; (c) the spread of disease introduced by the colonizer; (d) the use of the Indian and of his descendants as fodder for the canons in the wars of the Prata region and in the conflicts of rival factions of the dominant southern Rio Grandian class during the nineteenth century; (e) the expulsion to the city of the last descendants, who already had "become rather like a rustic type of white," where they died of malnutrition, from the beginning of the last century when they were already few in number. . . . Consequently, from an obviously different perspective, we can conclude, as did Moysés Vellinho, that the participation of the indigenous element in the genetic and sociocultural constitution of Rio Grande do Sul was "negligible."[22]

In his eagerness to demystify part of historiography, José Hildebrando Dacanal also negates the Indian's contribution to the formation of the southern Rio Grandian man. The argument is problematic, for, as Ligia Chiappini [Moraes Leite] points out, "If the process of the extinction of the Indian took place as he affirms, over three centuries, it is clear that during this time there could have been, and certainly was, miscegenation. In fact, he himself admits that this would have taken place among the lower classes when he centers the end of his essay on the negation of the phenomenon among the landowners who would have been primarily white and European."[23] Since neither Vellinho nor Dacanal worked with any research data that might have provided a foundation for their affirmations, one can only conclude that in both their visions, although from different perspectives, there is no place for the Indian in Rio Grande do Sul.

In the process of glorifying the Gaúcho, which is part of the social construction of his identity, it becomes necessary to distinguish him from his homonymous counterpart in other countries.

Thus in 1927, trying to describe the comparisons and contrasts between the Rio Grandian Gaúcho and the Gaúcho in general, Jorge Salis Goulart wrote:

The cruel Gaúcho is a creation of the Prata region Pampas. This sui generis type that fights merely for the love of fighting, eternal enemy of society and justice, untamable and adventurous warrior, dominated by the vice of gambling and by the love of bloody struggle, anonymous hero of the Pampas, this type is peculiar to the Spanish population. The Rio Grandian is not. He is sober, orderly, although he never fears confronting the enemy so that social organization may be maintained. The long series of bloody facts that the history of the Prata region registers is completely alien to the history of Rio Grande do Sul. . . . The Prata region Gaúcho is a rebel against society and the laws that govern it. The dictator who achieves supreme governance does not look for the good in people because he does not understand people. All the prerogatives in his personality are those of a rude and rustic autocrat. The Rio Grandian is just the opposite. In [18]35 he rebels to give his land a more secure government, more in accord with the necessities of his people.[24]

It is interesting that at the time these remarks were made, the Farroupilha Revolution (1835–1845) was only a few years away from its centennial and the wars of the Prata region had ended a long time before. What had happened recently in Rio Grande do Sul were internal conflicts of an extremely bloody and cruel nature.[25] Thus, from 1893 to 1895, the state was submerged in the Federalist Revolution, the "bloodiest civil war in Brazil's history; a war that lasted thirty-one months and produced ten to twelve thousand casualties in a state population of one million."[26] In this conflict, the two adversaries fought an extremely bloody war. The preferred manner of eliminating a prisoner was the ritual "beheading." The prisoner was made to kneel with his hands tied, and the executioner, with a sudden striking of the knife, would slash his throat (which was draped with colorful scarves that identified the prisoner's party affiliation), slashing from side to side, thus sectioning the carotid arteries much the same way one would kill sheep. A conservative estimate is that more than a thousand people were sacrificed in this way.[27] In 1923 a new internal conflict sprang up between the same groups involved in the Federalist Revolution.

One of the issues of the dispute was precisely the autocratic form of government of those in power who justified their dictatorial behavior on their interpretation, based on their own interests, of the positivist doctrine. The conflict ended with a pact that prohibited the state president from "electing himself" again. During that time the dictators were central figures in the state's conflicts and politics.

It may seem strange, therefore, to speak of the orderly character and peaceful nature of the Brazilian Gaúcho at such a time when Rio Grande do Sul had just experienced periods of extreme belligerence. At the same time one's attention is called to the constant preoccupation of Gaúcho historiography, from that time on, to emphasize the nonseparatist character of the Farroupilha Revolution. True, this preoccupation was already present on the occasion of the movement itself, which had as its origin the Rio Grandian landowners' lack of satisfaction with the excessive political centralization imposed by the central government and their belief that the province was being economically exploited by the rest of Brazil.[28] The revolt, against which the empire fought with more than half the national army, lasted almost ten years and ended only when the rebels agreed to amnesty. In 1838, Bento Gonçalves, landowner and leader of the *farrapos*,[29] published a manifesto to "civilized nations" arguing that the Rio Grandian Republic was a last gesture in the struggle against the intransigence of the empire. A classic episode is frequently evoked recounting the offer of troops by Rosas, the Argentine dictator, to the leader of the *farrapos*, David Canabarro. The latter is said to have rejected the offer with the following words: "Sir! The first of your soldiers who crosses the border will furnish the blood with which we will sign the Peace of Piratini with the empire, for even more important than our love for the Republic is our Brazilian honor."[30]

Part of historiography took up this same argument almost a century later. In 1923 an intellectual, in a speech on "The Separatist Ideology and the Rio Grandian Character," affirmed that "the revolutionaries wanted a republic, accepting the separation as an accidental means of achieving it. Never did the leaders of the memorable episode ever lose their feeling of national identity."[31] Another admired thinker, in a piece published at the beginning of the 1960s, affirmed that, "dragged by their serious difference of opinion with the empire, the revolutionaries went so far as to separate totally from the Republic; however, all this was still the work of Brazilians."[32] On 20 September 1935, the date of the Centennial of the Farroupilha Revolution, in a civic session sponsored in Rio de Janeiro by the government of the Federal District, a federal representative from Rio Grande do Sul gave a passionate speech in which he affirmed that, for the *farrapos*, the revolution "meant their ardent desire to establish a Brazilian identity; it was the feeling of Gaúcho patriotism, the confession that . . . they wanted to show they were Brazilian, that they wished to live within the Brazilian communion, linked by the Federation of the States. No one can darken this brilliant truth." Assuring that the rebels "were primarily, and above all, Brazilian," he concluded, "Oh, my Brazilian Rio Grande . . . It was for Brazil that we fought yesterday, that we fight today, and that we will fight tomorrow."[33]

More than the egregious omission in relation to what was actually occurring, what one notices in the writings of these intellectuals, when they insist on the nonseparatism of the Farroupilha Revolution and on the essential differences between the Brazilian Gaúcho and the one from the Prata region, is an attempt to affirm the Brazilian national identity of Rio Grande do Sul and its inhabitants. Although today this may seem superfluous, it is useful to remember that many of them were writing before or immediately after 1930, when the economic and political integration of the country was not yet solid. One of the central themes of intellectuals at the time was the formation of a national identity and a national integration. The 1930 Revolution, in as much as it meant a growing process of economic and political centralization, accentuated the idea of a national unity and attributed to the state the task of accomplishing it. It is necessary, therefore, not only to affirm the Brazilian identity of the Gaúcho but to emphasize his positive traits, even if in so doing it becomes necessary to make up reality, glossing over the elements that could eventually be considered "barbarian." These had to be "exported" to the other side of the border, to the Prata region.

It is significant that today the headquarters of the Legislative Assembly of Rio Grande do Sul is called Farroupilha Palace and that the headquarters of the state government, located next door, is called Piratini Palace, evoking the place that was the headquarters of the Rio Grandian Republic. Likewise, the anthem of Rio Grande do Sul is the anthem of the *farrapos*. In fact, the Farroupilha Revolution incorporated itself into the Rio Grandian symbology, being remembered and ritualized annually through a week that carries its name and that culminates with a state holiday on September 20, during which there are great parades by the troops of the State Brigade and the Centers for Gaúcho Traditions.

The peculiar relationship between Rio Grande do Sul and Brazil is evidenced symbolically in the state flag, which is composed of three colored stripes: one green, another yellow, each evoking the colors of the national flag, and a red stripe separating the two, denoting the blood that was spilled in the history of the state. In the middle of this red stripe, which symbolizes so passionately the quota of sacrifice paid by its inhabitants when they entered the federation, is a coat of arms that contains, among other objects, cannons, lances, bayonets, and two phrases—"Liberty, Equality, Humanity" (the motto of the *farrapos*) and "Rio Grandian Republic, 20 September 1835" (the date of the deflagration of the Farroupilha Revolution)—to serve as a constant reminder that, although Rio Grande do Sul may be part of Brazil, it was once an independent republic and that this fact must remain vivid in the collective memory of its citizens.[34]

Indeed, if we add the other conflicts involving Rio Grande do Sul to the struggles against the Spanish and the Farroupilha Revolution, an extremely bloody picture emerges. In the Paraguay War, which began twenty years after the end of the Farroupilha Revolution, almost a third of the Brazilian forces were soldiers from the state.[35] From 1893 to 1895 Rio Grande do Sul was involved in the Federalist Revolution mentioned above. In 1923 a new conflict arose between the same groups involved in the earlier war. The central government, adhering to the "governors' policy," did not intervene but served as a mediator in the conflict, which ended with the Pedras Altas Pact. It is interesting that the terms *federation* and *republic* are used ambiguously in these internal conflicts. Thus the members of the former Liberal Party, which dominated Gaúcho politics up until the Proclamation of the Republic, will find shelter within the Federalist Party. The group that succeeded in power, remaining there practically until 1930, was named the Rio-Grandian Republican Party, but its newspaper, which was fundamental to its actions, was curiously called *The Federation*. All this indicates once again that in the period from 1889 to 1930, a time marked by a new form of government (the Republic) and by political and administrative decentralization—a situation that differed from that of the empire which had a unitarian and centralizing policy—the question of how to belong to Brazil continued dramatically.

The state, in the current century, has been involved in a series of revolts and movements that were "pedagogical" in nature, through which the state intervened in national politics to provide another direction. Thus the "Prestes Column," which came to be one of the milestones of *tenentismo*, began in 1924 in Santo Angelo in the region of the Missions (almost at the Argentinian border) led by a young Rio Grandian captain in the National Army, Luiz Carlos Prestes, later general secretary of the Brazilian Communist Party. The march of the Prestes Column lasted more than two years, heading up to the Northeast (through Paraguay), so that upon returning through Goias and Mato Grosso, it ended in Bolivia in a trajectory that covered more than twenty-five thousand kilometers.

The 1930 Revolution, a movement that had as its origin the displeasure of the peripheral oligarchies and that placed Getúlio Vargas in power, also began in Rio Grande do Sul. The revolution was successful in making state politicians forget their local differences and face external problems together. It is significant that, once victorious, Getúlio Vargas moved to Rio de Janeiro, wearing a red scarf (the *federalist* symbol) around his neck—he, who had participated on the opposite side of the Republicans. This gesture symbolized simultaneously that the internal conflicts had ended and that, facing a larger problem, the state achieved peace to help solve the problems of Brazil. It is also noteworthy that the first speech Vargas gave when the Revolution occurred ended with the phrase "Rio Grande Standing Up for Brazil" and that this phrase was preceded by such remarks as "It was not in vain that our state achieved a sacred union" and "You cannot escape your heroic destiny!"[36] Making salient the role of vanguard that was attributed to the state in the moral regeneration of Brazil, Leite points out that the propaganda of the Liberal Alliance, primarily responsible for Getúlio Vargas's attaining power, and of the 1930 Revolution was founded "in the supposed physical and moral superiority of the Gaúcho, gained through the heroic struggles of the past and maintained until today, and in the belief that because he was the carrier of such ideal qualities, he is destined to the role of regenerator of the nation corrupted and destroyed by the successive plunderers of the Republic."[37]

In 1961, when President Jânio Quadros resigned and an attempt was made to block his vice president, the Rio Grandian Gaúcho João Goulart, from assuming the presidency, it was again in Rio Grande do Sul that a victorious resistance, which took the name "Legality," was enacted. The coup of 1964, although it had not originated in Rio Grande do Sul, would not have been possible without the participation of the then Third Army, headquartered in Porto Alegre, capital of the state—the army with the largest number of soldiers in Brazil. Of the five generals that governed the country from 1964 to 1985, three were Rio Grandian.

But if those episodes indicate that the intervention of Rio Grande do Sul in national politics was needed to correct its direction, it is interesting that frequently Rio Grandians continue to complain that the state did not profit at all by this intervention. Once again, the state would be losing in its relationship with Brazil. Thus, on the occasion of the sesquicentennary of the Farroupilha Revolution, the then minister of agriculture and later the governor of Rio Grande do Sul made the following statement:

> Our marginalization in the national political life has both recent and more remote causes. The recent ones are well known: many of our leaders were, in the last twenty some years, intimately associated with the regime that has now ended. The discrediting of the past regime naturally extended itself to this Rio Grandian leadership. More serious, however, was the fact that the aforementioned leadership participated in high federal administrative positions without positing a well-defined defense project or a stimulus for the development of Rio Grande. We received the discredit but did not increase our participation in the national decision-making process. . . . The manner in which Rio Grande participates in the national life is anchored in difficulties that began long ago. I refer to the traditional manner in which Rio Grande has been included in national politics. Our participation in political life has oscillated between two extremes. On the one hand, we have shown a tendency toward a certain exclusion, toward isolating ourselves; on the other hand, we have participated peripherally in the central system of power. With the revolution of 1930, our best political and administrative figures emigrated to the center of the country and occupied high positions in the federal administration. The project of modernization that was begun at that time, however, did not consider that Rio Grande

deserved to be rewarded in a manner equivalent to our contribution to the future direction of the state machinery.[38]

The sesquicentennary of the Farroupilha Revolution was an amply commemorated historical marker. But, contrary to what had happened fifty years earlier, the emphasis was on the differences between the state and Brazil, and not between the state and Argentina or Uruguay. This can only be understood by taking several factors into account. First, consider the fact that Brazil is strongly integrated economically and politically, as well as in terms of transportation, mass communication networks, and so on. In this sense, national integration clearly occurred. In fact, from 1930 on there was increasing centralization, giving the state more and more power. It is no longer necessary, therefore, to emphasize how much Rio Grande do Sul belongs to Brazil. On the contrary, in 1985 the state, acting in a similar manner as it had 150 years before, became "estranged" from Brazil for it considered itself wronged and its honor hurt.

This brings us to the second factor accounting for the so-called crisis in Rio Grande do Sul, which reached its climax around 1985. Several events came together and were called a crisis. Recent history of the state has shown a strong feeling of marginalization based on the supposed loss of economic and political importance with regard to the rest of the country. In a sense, the discourse is a restatement, on the part of the economic and political elite, of the *farroupilha* complaints formulated 150 years ago.[39]

The crisis and marginalization discourse, which is constantly being brought up to date in the history of Rio Grande do Sul, appears today, for example, at the political level in the form of a complaint that with the end of the military cycle, Rio Grande do Sul was left with few ministries when in the previous governments it had many. This obviously must be analyzed further, since the presence of several ministries in the federal government from 1964 to 1985 did not mean that it had adopted policies favoring the state.

On the economic level, the complaint centers around the loss of economic vitality. What happened, in truth, is somewhat different. Despite the occurrence, from the 1930s on, of a growing centralization of resources and power on the part of the federal government and the concentration of industry in São Paulo, Rio Grande do Sul has not fared so badly. Besides the political influences it always had, economically the state continues to be rich and productive. In the last thirty years, industry acquired a central importance in the state economy, representing 7.2 percent of the country's total industrial production. The state is responsible for 12 percent of Brazilian exports and for 10 percent of Brazil's gross national product. Moreover, Rio Grande do Sul has the best national health indexes (the lowest mortality rate and the highest life-expectancy rate) and the lowest indexes of illiteracy (13.5 percent). Its economic growth indicators have closely followed those of the country and have reflected the national fluctuations. Thus "the most accurate characterization of the present-day Gaúcho economic situation is that its problems are not manifestations of a regional crisis, but rather regional consequences of a severe national crisis."[40]

What has been labeled a crisis also has to do with the difficulties confronting the state government. The state apparatus is incapable of securing resources that might enable it to confront the administrative deals previously made, thus leaving the state unable to pay its public workers, whose numbers almost tripled in the 1960s to the 1980s to almost twice that of the state of Paraná. Thus the state frequently has to borrow money, and in 1986 it had the greatest debt of all state governments. It is important to remember, however, that the majority of Brazilian states are extremely indebted and that the governors who took office in 1987 began to recover a greater portion of the taxes secured by the federal government, a situation that was contemplated in the 1988 Constitution.

Another element contributing to what has been called the crisis has to do with the intervention of the Central Bank in the private financial institutions of Rio Grande do Sul, which were at the brink of bankruptcy. Although justified, the federal government's action was seen as yet another intervention in state affairs and again brought to light a feeling of revolt. In one case, that dealing with the Sulbrasileiro Bank, which occurred at the end of the military regime, the intervention provoked a reaction that succeeded in the new federal government reopening the bank in 1985, with a new name and composition and with public financing. The movement that mobilized different social groups, from bank clerks to owners of local corporations, brought about a regional discourse and appealed to a symbology that was strongly related to traditional Gaúcho values. In downtown Porto Alegre, one could see many people dressed in *bombachas* (traditional baggy pants worn by the

Gaúcho) on horseback as a form of protest against what was perceived as discrimination against the state. Members of a new
movement, suggestively called "Get it up Gaúcho," camped in a
park in the capital awaiting a resolution to the banking crisis and
arrived in a caravan at the headquarters of the Sulbrasileiro Bank in
the middle of the downtown area. One of the group's leaders, a cattle rancher, declared that "Rio Grande do Sul owes much less to
Brazil than Brazil owes us."[41] The same person made an appeal
from the movement for everyone to close out their accounts in
banks outside the state and to transfer their money to regional
banks. This type of bizarre outcry sounds strange at the very least
when, as a journalist aptly observed, "Those who eventually tore
up the money belts of their compatriots were precisely two gen-
uinely Gaúcho banks."[42]

The image of suffering that Brazil was imposing on Rio Grande
do Sul and the public declaration of the need to take drastic measures that in the end could even mean separation became relatively
frequent. Thus in 1984 the then secretary of justice in the state saw
to the publication of the "Letter to the Liberators" (members of the
extinct Liberation Party, successor of the former Federalist Party
and favorable to the parliamentary regime) in which he stated,
"The Federation is a farce! Financial centralism is making the
states insolvent. Our Rio Grande is suffering, its vocation of growing through work disturbed, and the pride of its fighting people,
reduced to the condition of beggars, is hurt. *We have never favored
a divisionist spirit, but today's reasons are stronger than those in
1935.*"[43]

In a more explicit gesture, a well-known photographer published
a tongue-in-cheek article in a magazine with the largest circulation
in Brazil, proposing the proclamation of a Gaúcho Republic.
According to him:

> Separatism is not only in fashion—it is in the blood of the
> Gaúcho. In the Chimarrão circles [ritualized drinking of a bitter
> tea called *mate*, served in gourds and drunk through a silver
> straw], in the weekend barbecues, in the straight track races [cus-
> tom of racing nonpedigreed horses on an improvised track], the
> subject always calls attention and initiates polemic. Today Rio
> Grande do Sul always appears in the Brazilian news as a beggar
> for federal alms, crying the pain of a national crisis that we did
> not help to bring about, but, on the contrary, one we tried to

appease with our export of grain and diversified industrial production. The time has come for us to be more in favor of ourselves and once again to raise the flag of the Rio Grandian
Republic, independent and sovereign.[44]

In May 1990, in a public act that took place in the dependencies
of the Legislative Assembly of Rio Grande do Sul, there was an
attempt to create the Party of the Farroupilha Republic. The
spokesman for the movement, the attorney Antônio Carlos Estrela,
argued that "the Federative Republic of Brazil is a state that did not
work and we are going to fight for the right of Brazilian people and
federated states to constitute themselves as sovereign states."
Estrela proposed "to articulate the separatist cause throughout Rio
Grande do Sul, a state that would be fused with Santa Catarina and
possibly also engage the support of Paraná, and these three states
would begin to adopt their own development models."[45] The public act was attended by a mere fifty people, a fact that did not stop
the then senator and later minister of justice, Jarbas Passarinho,
from writing an article condemning the movement.[46]

The year 1990 also saw the publication of the book, *Vai nascer
um novo país; República do pampa gaúcho. União dos estados de
Santa Catarina e Rio Grande do Sul*, by Irton Marx.[47] The author
is the son of German descendants and lives in Santa Cruz do Sul, a
city colonized by Germans. He began by proposing that the states
of Rio Grande do Sul and Santa Catarina separate, to be joined afterward by the state of Paraná. His book is a mixture of proposals that
may be seen as a gathering of magical solutions for the diffuse dissatisfaction of certain sectors in Rio Grande do Sul. The author
begins by speaking of the evils that attack the world, such as greed,
avarice, selfishness, unemployment, the disorderly growth in population and cities, crime, and so on. He goes on to speak of the loss
of hope in the South with the rest of Brazil and of the need to create a Republic of the Gaúcho Pampa. The program this new country would heed is given in extreme detail: besides being obsessively
preoccupied with cleanliness, it presumes that reality can be
changed through laws and good will. The program has racist connotations against blacks who should stop "the cult of systems and
folklore that are rather primitive" and "learn to be more careful
and not throw their money away." The program favors the immigration of people from Nordic, German, Japanese, Italian, Polish, or

Slavic regions, "because they have already proven their capacity in our country."[48]

In 1993 Marx achieved national and international notoriety when Globo Television Network, the largest television network in Brazil, aired a program about his movement and interviewed him. Since, according to the Brazilian constitution, Brazil is a federative republic formed by the indivisible union of its states and municipalities, the federal police felt compelled to indict him based on the Law of National Security which characterizes as a crime the attempt to dismember a part of the national territory. This gave Marx even greater notoriety. Since at the time the world was very attentive to separatist movements and to the wars that resulted from those efforts, as seen in the former Yugoslavia, the world press began to pay attention to Irton Marx. In 1993 he announced that he was going to proclaim the Federal Republic of the Gaúcho Pampa, comprising the states of Rio Grande do Sul, Santa Catarina, and Paraná. I was in Santa Cruz do Sul on 22–23 May 1993, during the weekend the Republic was to be proclaimed, and I had the opportunity to interview Irton Marx. He ended up not showing up at the central plaza in the city where the proclamation was to take place, alleging that were he to appear he would be arrested by the police, and therefore the Republic was not proclaimed. By my calculations, the maximum number of people at the central plaza, including curiosity seekers and the many journalists who came to cover the event, was never more than three hundred. After the failure to proclaim the Federal Republic of the Gaúcho Pampa, the movement lost its momentum.

Marx is considered an ambiguous figure by many of the people I interviewed in Santa Cruz do Sul. He lives with his mother; at times he claims to be single, at other times he claims to be separated. He calls himself a sociologist, but no one knows where he studied. In his book he claims to be part of the military, but apparently he merely completed the compulsory military service. It is not clear how he makes his living; he has been involved in several ventures that did not succeed. This position outside the mainstream gives him the ability to represent, in a demoralized and histrionic way, what some feel in a latent form and cannot formulate.

Perhaps it is precisely because so few people today are seriously thinking about separating Rio Grande do Sul from Brazil that this idea can be voiced as an arrogant threat or in a tongue-in-cheek manner. Again, we are addressing the unique relationship that exists between Brazil and its southernmost state, as well as the tension this relationship promotes.

At the same time there are limits to affirming that the state is in crisis because of the risk of creating an image that presents the situation as insurmountable. Moreover, in this same sense, how can one even propose a separate republic (even if only as a threat or a rhetorical suggestion) if the state's image is negative?

Thus it is interesting to note that even though at a certain moment (the sesquicentennary of the Farroupilha Revolution) the titles of articles, editorials, reports, and publicity in newspapers and magazines were quite apocalyptic and pessimist ("The Economic Decline of Rio Grande," "RS in a Crisis of Being Discredited," "Rio Grande Is No Longer What It Once Was"),[49] immediately afterward the same periodicals changed their discourse to an integrationist and optimistic register ("Save Rio Grande?" "There Are More Than Plenty of Reasons to Believe More and More in Rio Grande," "Rio Grande do Sul Is Already Beginning to Change").[50] A journalist even published an article entitled "Rio Grande Becomes Not Viable" and published another nine months later entitled "Rio Grande Is Viable."[51]

This relationship of autonomy and isolation brings about a discourse affirming that Rio Grande do Sul is simultaneously in a situation of calamity and of great vitality. What demands our attention is how the themes that occupy the Gaúcho population recur at such different times. The peculiarities of the state and its fragile relationship with the rest of Brazil are constantly being evoked and brought up to date. Rio Grande do Sul may be seen as a state where regionalism is constantly reposited in new historical, economic, and political situations. However, although the junctures may be new and the fashion of the discourse modernized, the basic substrata on which these discourses rest is surprisingly similar. In this sense one can affirm that Gauchism is a well-developed case of regionalism, inasmuch as it is able to articulate political claims common to an entire state. The continuity and vitality of this regionalist discourse indicate that the messages it evokes strongly conform to representations of Gaúcho identity.

Attempt to Proclaim the Federal Republic of the Gaúcho Pampa, 22–23 May 1993

1. Separatists prepare the scene. The Banner says "Pampa My Country. Separatist Movement." Courtesy of Andréa Fachel Leal

2. Separatists wearing *bombachas* and boots carrying the flag of the Pampa Federal Republic. The poster in the background reads: "Pampa Republic. Plebiscite Now!" Courtesy of Andréa Fachel Leal

3. The curious gather in the central square of Santa Cruz do Sul where the Federal Republic of the Gaúcho Pampa was to be proclaimed. The banner says: "Pampa Republic. Adopt This New Fatherland."
Courtesy of Andréa Fachel Leal

4. Separatists with the flag of the Pampa Republic. The banner reads: "Give Them Separatism"(in the sense of"Give Them Hell,"referring to Central Brazil). The T-shirts read: "Pampa My Country."
Courtesy of Andréa Fachel Leal

5. Separatists, the curious, and journalists. The banner in the background reads: "Separatist Movement of the Federal Republic of the Pampa." Courtesy of Andréa Fachel Leal

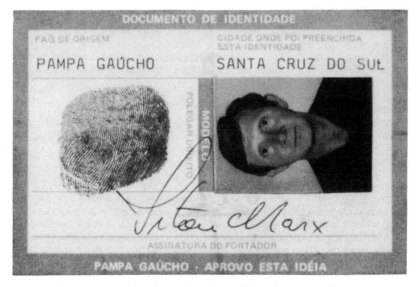

6. Identification Card for the Federal Republic of the Gaúcho Pampa with the photograph of its creator, Irton Marx. The card says "Identification Document. Country of origin: Gaúcho Pampa. City where this ID was issued: Santa Cruz do Sul. Right thumb fingerprint. Signature. Gaúcho Pampa. I approve of this idea." Courtesy of Sylvio Sirangelo

Chapter Four

IN SEARCH OF A LOST TIME: THE GAÚCHO TRADITIONALIST MOVEMENT

•

The image one has at the mention of Gaúcho traditions—whatever the perspective of the person describing it—always has at its roots vast open plains, more specifically in the pastoral latifundia *Campanha* (located in the Southwest of Rio Grande do Sul and bordering Argentina and Uruguay); the image of the Gaúcho, of course, is that of a free and errant man who travels as a sovereign on his horse. The Gaúcho's only interlocutor is nature as it reveals itself on the spacious plains of this pastoral area of the state. This idea of fearlessness and daring that is linked to the inhabitants of the Pampa region is clearly expressed in the words of one of the last Gaúcho leaders who came from the *Campanha*:

> This is my region and is also my life. Whoever is born in these endless plains has to have an open mind, has to fight loyally, has to confront nature and man with a clean consciousness. An influential element in one's psychology, in one's way of life, in one's manner of facing others and facing oneself, this Pampa is the soul and heart of the Gaúcho from the frontier region.[1]

From the eighteenth century, when Rio Grande do Sul began its colonization, until the Farroupilha Revolution from 1835 to 1845, the southwestern region of the state was "a region whose borders were perfectly confused with the limits of the province, since the *Campanha* constituted the only Gaúcho space effectively appropriated and incorporated into the national economy. In the words of Jean Roche, 'Rio Grande do Sul was the Pampa.' "[2] However, the emergence of a strong contingent of small farmers and merchants who were descendants of German and Italian immigrants in the northern half of the state, as well as the cattle crisis that began around 1870, posed a serious threat to the economic and political hegemony of the *Campanha*.

Sérgio da Costa Franco points out that "a good portion of the Brazilian compatriots identify Rio Grande do Sul with the sociocultural characteristics of the *Campanha*, ignoring the fact that nowadays this region occupies a second-tier position in the economic picture of the state. The *Campanha* has lost its demographic hegemony, and consequently its political dominance, and is an area marked by the darkest corners of underdevelopment."[3]

In spite of the decadence of the *Campanha*,[4] and of the growth of other regions in the state—like the mountainous region of German and Italian colonization—the figure of the Gaúcho, with his country expressions that include his horse, his *Chimarrão*, and the construction of a free and brave social type, also served as a model for different ethnic groups. This image of the Gaúcho unites the inhabitants of the state and juxtaposes the state with the rest of the country.

Consider the following cultlike observations of these traditions. First, in the middle of the nineteenth century, the marginal figure of the Gaúcho, as one pictures him in the past, no longer existed because of certain transformations—the Gaúcho's gradual incorporation as a ranch worker. Around 1870 the state experienced economic shifts, characterized by the fencing off of fields, the appearance of new cattle groups, and the dissemination of a network of transportation. These changes meant a great modernization of the *Campanha*, simplifying cattle-raising activities and eliminating certain menial tasks such as that of the *posteiro*, who kept the cattle within the boundaries of the ranch, and that of the indentured servant, who ended up largely being expelled from the fields. The appearance of foreign firms that used cold-storage techniques and the decadence of the meat-drying processing plants accentuated this trend after the end of World War I, when one begins to delineate the figure of the "Gaúcho on foot" (no longer on horseback), to borrow the expression coined by the writer Cyro Martins in his social novels.[5]

According to Sergius Gonzaga, at around the middle of the nineteenth century the marginalized type of Gaúcho was practically extinct and consequently apt to reappear as an instrument of ideological sustenance, imposed by the very groups that had destroyed him. Thus in 1868, at the time of the Paraguay War, a group of intellectuals and writers in Porto Alegre, capital of Rio Grande do Sul, founded the Literary Parthenon, a society of intellectuals and men of letters that tried to join European cultural models with the positivistic vision of the Rio Grandian oligarchy through the exaltation of the regional Gaúcho. According to Gonzaga:

> It is up to the members of the Parthenon Society to praise the representative types that were dearest to the ruling class. This is the beginning of the eulogies for the heroic figures who were elevated as symbols of the grandeur of the Rio Grandian people. We find in the Farroupilha revolt the paradigms of honor, liberty, and equality that would become inherent in the future Gaúcho myth. This myth dissolved the economic motives and class differences that existed in the conflict. The hero configuration was not yet that of the stylized and glamorized Gaúcho, but the laudatory vector was already present. One sees the praise through the appearance in cities, especially in Porto Alegre, of "enlightened" young men—originally from the middle class—who would use literature as the springboard for their upward climb. We saw a repetition of the national phenomenon: the social mobility of this intelligentsia from dubious origins was related to how close they were with those in power. An exchange was articulated: upward mobility, prestige, or mere recognition was exchanged for sub-ideologues, those capable of offering formulas (amenable to the oligarchy) for the representation of reality; these rewards were also exchanged for artists capable of putting in prose and verse the virile qualities of this same oligarchy.[6]

The Literary Parthenon contributed to the exaltation of the Gaúcho written by scholars, and it is at the end of the nineteenth century that the first traditionalist society appeared. This society, the Gaúcho *Grêmio* (literally, a bosom or a close-knit group with a common goal) of Porto Alegre turned to traditions through the promotion of parties, parades of horsemen, sponsored lectures, and so on. The group was founded in 1898 by the Positivist Republican João Cezimbra Jacques, a man of modest origins who had been a volunteer soldier in the Paraguay War and ended his military career as a major in the National Army. The idea of founding this association came to him with the following specific objective:

> Organizing the calendar of commemorations of great happenings in our land . . . [w]e believe that this patriotic group is not intended to maintain in a modern society those customs that have been abolished by our natural evolution and that cannot belong to the time in which we live. Nor do we believe that this association has as its goal the practice of games and other recreational elements that do belong to the present time and that are imported from abroad. Neither one nor the other. It is an association destined to maintain the character of our great state and consequently of our great traditions by means of regular commemorations of dates and facts that made the Southern Rio Grandian people famous not only nationally but internationally. We will achieve this goal by means of celebrations and parties that do not exclude usage and customs, games, or diversions of the present time and that illustrate, whenever possible, good usages and customs, games, and diversions of the past. We plan celebrations that not only remind us of and praise notable facts through words and speech, but also do so through popular songs, dances, exercises, and worthy practices in which the participants wear appropriate clothing and carry props that are those used by the Gaúcho.[7]

Besides emphasizing the cult of traditions, the quote above poses questions already salient at the time and ones that will be posed again later: the existence of customs that have been surpassed by "our natural evolution," the problem of practices brought from "abroad," the existence of "good" uses and customs, and so on.

We must point out two things in common between the Literary Parthenon and the Gaúcho Association. Both groups are made up of people of modest origins who possess neither land nor capital and who find in intellectual activities a form of upward mobility and integration into the power structure. It is an incipient group of intellectuals that finds itself in a period of gestation and will inevitably become glued to power, as occurred in other parts of Brazil and in the world. Economic, social, and political conditions do not yet exist for this group to achieve a relative autonomous status. Similar to joining the army and participating in political activities, the pursuit of intellectual activities is one of the few forms of upward social mobility for these dispossessed classes in society.

The second aspect is that both associations, although in different ways, were preoccupied with questions of tradition and modernity. The Parthenon, while its literary model is an educated Europe and all the most advanced ideas that such a group could offer, evokes the traditional figure of the Gaúcho and worships his values that were being disturbed. The Gaúcho Association, in the words of its founder, tries to maintain traditions without excluding present-day customs. In both associations we find as a backdrop a state that is beginning to change and where tension between the past and the present is beginning to appear.

The year the Gaúcho Association was created is the same in which the Positivist Republican leader Borges de Medeiros began his first term as president of Rio Grande do Sul, a post he occupied for almost thirty years. With the proclamation of the Republic, the Rio Grandian Republican Party assumed power in the state. Although also belonging to the economic elite, its members did not belong to the cattle ranch oligarchy of the *Campanha*. Quite the contrary, the majority were from the North. The group that took power was formed by young people who had obtained university degrees in São Paulo and Rio de Janeiro and who had a modernizing and authoritarian project based on their reading of Positivism. This reading came from the idea that an enlightened despotism was the best strategy for organizing society. Auguste Comte favored the existence of "small fatherlands" with populations lower than three million (Rio Grande do Sul at the time of the proclamation of the Republic had about a million people). Comte's idea was interpreted by the Brazilian positivists as the defense of a radical federalism since at the time the provinces did not have the means of becoming independent. For Júlio de Castilhos, the founder and ideologue of the Rio Grandian Republican Party, this implied "the nonrecognition of not simply one Brazilian nation, but of several Brazilian nations provisionally organized under a federation, each state able to organize itself independently in a republican form without any limitations by the Federal Constitution."[8]

Adhering to the Positivist idea that progress can only be obtained through order, Júlio de Castilhos had as his motto "conserve while improving." Shortly before the proclamation of the Republic, writing in the newspaper *The Federation*, official propaganda organ of his party, Castilhos defended the celebration of September 20 (the day the Farroupilha Revolution began in 1835) as the "Day of the Gaúcho": "The commemoration of September 20 has . . . an ideal that means that the past is the source which inspires the present to direct the ways of the future." After the Republic was proclaimed and after his party assumed power in Rio Grande do Sul, Júlio de Castilhos wrote a state constitution, with a strong Positivist inspiration, that defined as "the official insignia of the state the tricolor flag of the ill-fated Rio Grandian Republic." It is significant that this dialectic between the old and the new, the past and the present, tradition and modernity, is ever present in the processes we are analyzing.

After the founding of the Gaúcho Association, several other traditionalist entities followed: the Gaúcho Union of Pelotas (founded in 1899 by the great regionalist writer Simões Lopes Neto), the Gaúcho Center of Bagé (founded in 1899), the Gaúcho Association of Santa Maria (founded in 1901), the Gaúcho Society of Lomba Grande (founded in 1938 in the area of German colonization), and the Farroupilha Club of Ijuí (founded in 1943 in the area of German and Italian colonization). These six entities are generally considered "pioneer" movements by the traditionalists.[9]

The first Center for Gaúcho Traditions (*Centro de Tradições Gauchas*), or " '35 CTG," was founded in 1948 in Porto Alegre. The name '35 CTG evokes the Farroupilha Revolution which began in 1835. This center will serve as a model for the hundreds of other traditional centers located in Rio Grande do Sul and in several other states in Brazil and abroad. The majority of the founding members of these centers were high school students who came from the interior of the country, primarily from the pastoral areas where there was a predominance of cattle raising in the tradition of the large latifundia.

The creation of the '35 CTG was preceded by the founding, in 1947, by the same young people, of the Department of Gaúcho Traditions of the Student Association of the Júlio de Castilhos Public School. Júlio de Castilhos was considered at the time the model public school where the majority of these young people studied. They organized the first *Ronda Gaúcha* [Gaúcho Festival] (today Farroupilha Week), which took place that year from September 7, Brazilian Independence Day, to September 20, the day the 1835 Farroupilha Revolution began. Taking a spark from the symbolic flame of the Fatherland's Bonfire (*Pira da Pátria*) before it was extinguished at midnight on September 7, they transported it to the atrium of the Júlio de Castilhos School where they lit the "*Creole* Flame"[10] in a bunkhouse lamp. Thus the flame was used to build a symbolic relationship between the independence of Brazil and the attempt at independence by the state of Rio Grande do Sul.

That same year the National Defense League included among its festivities for Fatherland Week (the week-long celebration commemorating the anniversary of Brazil's independence), the transfer of the remains of General David Canabarro, the second man in the Farroupilha Revolution, from Santana do Livramento, the municipality in the *Campanha* region where he had been a cattle rancher, to the Pantheon of the Brotherhood of the Holy House of Mercy in Porto Alegre. Eight of these young men organized an honor guard (with horses obtained with the help of the Military Brigade, the official designation of the military police in Rio Grande Do Sul) to accompany the remains of the Farroupilha hero. This episode appears in several of the traditionalist documents as a fundamental rite of passage and as a myth of creation of the Gaúcho Traditionalist Movement (GTM).

Barbosa Lessa, one of the founders, recounts that, having come from the interior to study in Porto Alegre, he wanted to find the monument of Bento Gonçalves on horseback. Barbosa Lessa greatly admired this hero of the Farroupilha Revolution:

> And to my great surprise (I asked five or six people), no one knew where the monument was located, until someone said, "Oh, it's on João Pessoa Avenue," near where I used to study. I went to see the Bento Gonçalves Monument—this was in 1945—and I found that the monument looked abandoned. Then I spoke to Bento Gonçalves, "Hey old man, you look quite abandoned, quite forgotten, but I promise that I will make sure you are remembered. On September 20 lots of people will parade through here to honor you."[11]

Two years later, on 5 September 1947, the same Barbosa Lessa continues to recount:

I was at home in the morning reading the newspaper and I read that the remains of David Canabarro were arriving. Then I went outside and started running; I still had time to get to the event, right there in the *Praça da Alfândega* [Customs Plaza, in downtown Porto Alegre] to join in the applause for the arrival of the remains of David Canabarro. To my surprise I saw some young men about my age, on horseback, dressed in the Gaúcho fashion, participating in the event of the National Defense League. There were speeches and the like, and when the group scattered, I ran after them and asked the one that looked like the leader, a thin chap with a huge mustache: "Who are you? How can I be part of your group?" Then the chap said: "Look, you can look for me, I'm studying at Júlio de Castilhos." I said, "Gee! I'm studying at Júlio de Castilhos also." "But I'm studying at night," he said. "I'm also a night student. What is your name?" "Paixão [Côrtes]." "I'm Lessa."[12]

Interviews with some of these founders, who continue to be prominent figures in the Gaúcho Traditionalist Movement, reveal that most of them are descendants of small rural landowners from the pastoral latifundia area or sons of ranchers who found themselves in the process of downward social mobility and who had come to the capital to study. This information is significant because it shows that the founders of the GTM, although they espouse the values linked to the latifundia, do not originate from the rural oligarchy. This is also evidence that traditionalism, from its very beginnings, was an urban movement that tried to recoup the rural values of the past. As one of its intellectuals observes: "There is, whether we like it or not, an aura of wistfulness and longing involving traditionalism; no one misses those who are nearby. Longing—and traditionalism—demand a distancing, so much so that this is a city phenomenon, not a countryside phenomenon, urban, not rural."[13]

The capital, where these young men came to complete their studies, living with relatives and having to study at night and work during the day, was in contrast to their lives in their own hometowns, which posed both a threat and a challenge at the same time. In the words of one of these young men:

Porto Alegre fascinated us with its neon signs; Hollywood made us dizzy with the Technicolor beauty of Gene Tierney and the adventures of Tyrone Power; record stores filled our ears with the irresistible harmonies of Harry James and Tommie Dorsey, but down very deep, we preferred the security that only our "little corner of the world" knew how to offer, in the solidarity of friends, in the happiness of saddling a horse, and in the convivial intimacy of the rounds in the bunkhouse. We did not know one another, but we must have run into one another in the labyrinths of the capital. We had never heard about the old nativist[14] experiences of the sixties, the nineties, and the twenties—and we needed to choose our own directions by ourselves. And when Jean-Paul Sartre's existentialism presented to us a defeatist idea, as well as one of disbelief, instinctively we held on to our rough ancestors for an affirmation of victory and faith. Around this time, Rio Grande had all but been forgotten; even the state flag remained burned and hidden since November 1937—residues of the New State and its centralizing stranglehold.[15]

These words are valuable because of the information they offer. First, there is the description of the city. Although Porto Alegre in the 1940s was a small and peaceful city by today's standards, its population had increased from 272,000 inhabitants in 1940 to 394,000 by 1950 (a growth of 45 percent in ten years). It was seen as a metropolis filled with labyrinths and symbols of progress, such as the neon signs. Second, there were the products of the cultural industry arriving from the United States, which had a great impact through records and movies and their idols. Finally, we are told of the effect of skeptic philosophies from Europe that questioned the meaning of life and of the world. All this was fascinating, but at the same time very threatening. The reaction of these rural young men exposed to these experiences was to hold on to what they considered secure and apparent: the countryside and the past. There were two threats hovering over these values: the cultural innovations that would come via the United States (it should be remembered that during World War II there was a strong penetration of U.S. cultural products, such as Disney magazines and films, Hollywood cinema, Coca-Cola, and so on)[16] and the economic, political, and cultural centralism imposed by the dictatorship of the New State.

On 24 April 1948, a group of twenty-four young people composed of students from the Júlio de Castilhos Public School and a group of former Boy Scouts somewhat older and already working for the most part as salespeople, created the '35 CTG. After some discussion about the type of association it would be, the idea was suggested to transform it into a kind of traditionalist academy restricted to thirty-five members, but it was decided that the association would be open to all who wished to participate.

The group, made up exclusively of young men, began to meet every Saturday afternoon in an improvised bunkhouse[17] at the parents' home of one of the members. They met to drink *mate* tea and imitate the habits of the interior, sharing the kind of talk the farmhands used to have in the bunkhouses at the ranches:

> We would meet around a bonfire at Duque de Caxias Street to tell stories. Only young men. Women did not belong to the group, since usually in the bunkhouse it was only men . . . We cherished our meetings here as if we were in the *Campanha*, drinking our *Chimarrão*; sometimes even a little rum would appear. Each one would pitch in a few coins, thus contributing toward the purchase of the *mate*—minimal expenses. We did not have many pretensions of revolutionizing the world, although we did not agree with the type of civilization that was imposed on us from all sides . . . we did not intend to write about the Gaúcho or about the bunkhouse: from the first moment, we became the figure of the Gaúcho, dressing, speaking like the Gaúcho, and we felt ourselves owners of the world when we met on Saturday afternoons around the bonfire.[18]

It is obvious that this group is exclusively male and reproduces the world of the cattle farm in the *Campanha* where men are in the majority. Women were only later integrated into traditionalism and in a subaltern fashion.

Although at first the young men did not intend to become a group that would reflect on tradition but rather to be a group that tried to live it, they needed to re-create what they imagined to be the customs of the countryside. Thus the internal structure of the '35 CTG did not use the nomenclature that normally exists in associations but adopted the names used in the administration of a pastoral establishment, since the youth wanted to evoke a ranchlike environment. Instead of a president, vice president, secretary, treasurer, director, and so on, they took the titles of boss, foreman, vice foreman, servants, herdsman, and so forth. Instead of a deliberating or consulting council, they had a council of cowboys, and instead of departments, they created *invernadas* [the name given to the

large land areas fenced off in the ranches and used for fattening cat-
tle]. Similarly, all cultural, civic, or field activities received names
that had their origins in the customs of the Gaúcho ranches, such
as rounds, round-ups, rodeos, and so on.[19]

The statutes of the '35 CTG affirmed that the center shall have
the following goals:

a. to care for the traditions of Rio Grande do Sul, its history, its legends, songs, customs, and so on, and consequently their dissemination throughout the sister states and neighboring countries;
b. to fight for increasingly greater moral and cultural standards for
Rio Grande do Sul;
c. to foster the creation of regionalist groups in the state, giving
them all possible support. The center will not develop any kind of
political partisan, racial, or religious activities.[20]

It was a surprise to the founders who had opted for an association
open to all sectors that social origin soon became a consideration:

As the number of young students grew, even during the first
moments of the movement, the young men from a better socioeconomic position—sons of ranchers or those who were already
ranchers—began to leave the movement. It became a movement
of poor young men because . . . the richer kids did not want to mix
with the masses. As a result, we watched the young men leaving
us who were in the best position to help us, who had the means
of bringing horses, of contributing to a building fund. The rest of
us, those who survived on a very small salary, took our turn at
contributing, even after paying for our studies and everything
else, each of us bringing something—if I'm not mistaken it was
Glaucus [Saraiva] who called it "the horn of plenty." It was a
horn, a cuplike horn, that made the rounds and each of us would
give a few coins that were used to buy *Chimarrão*, and so on.[21]

Although they did not have among their membership the sons of
the ranchers, the second place the '35 CTG met was the headquarters of the FARSUL (Federation of Rural Associations of Rio Grande
do Sul, today the Agricultural Federation of the State of Rio Grande
do Sul), an organ representing the ranchers. In the same way that
the ranchers' sons showed discrimination in not wanting to be
involved with the CTG, so too the people from the state capital did
not prove very receptive to traditionalism:

It is not that Porto Alegre did not receive us well. After all, we were young, nice, happy, communicative, hard workers and good students, and the citizenry of the capital had no reason to hate us. But it was a city whose citizens were very conscious of their responsibility to be the transmitters of cosmopolitan culture and consumerism, and they had no time to waste with our chats and recitals. The most that they did was to smile condescendingly during our parades, when we carried our Creole Flame on September 20—an occasion that revitalized us because we saw we were no longer just a half-dozen alley-cats but that we numbered closer to a dozen young men. Maybe even two dozen.[22]

The complaint against the citizens of the capital and the state's elite for their rejection of the movement is a constant among the traditionalist leadership. This leadership resents the fact that the success of the movement is not recognized and that traditionalism continues to be seen as "a red-neck activity."

It is significant that the next CTG, the *Fogão Gaúcho* [Gaúcho stove], appeared on 7 August 1948 in Taquara, a city in the area of German colonization, leaving the traditionalists puzzled:

We tried to publicize our activities; according to the statutes we were required to publicize our traditions to neighboring countries and sister states. We believed that our expansion would come from other states. But the first response for another CTG came from Taquara, the region of German colonization. This confused all of our objectives. We thought that the response would certainly come from the *Campanha* but instead it came from the region of German colonization.[23]

In contrast to the founders of the '35 CTG who were all young students from the interior, descendants of small rural landowners from the latifundia, and practically all with Portuguese last names,[24] the founders of the second CTG were adults, and a great many of them were of German origin. Similarly to what may have occurred with the first two pioneer CTGs created in the area of German colonization during World War II, the creation of the CTG in Taquara was a way that its founders could reaffirm their Brazilian national identity and their Gaúcho identity. Interviews with some of the founders suggest a relationship between World War II and the creation of the association, indicating a "need some of the participants of the Chimarrão circle had to reaffirm, before Taquara society, that they were Gaúcho and not foreigners. Since many of them, being of German descent, still felt the pangs associated with the persecution they suffered during World War II when they were suspected of belonging to the Fifth Column[25] . . . this desire may not have been the intention of the majority of those who associated with the CTG after its founding, but it certainly was the intention of some of the new associates."[26]

The appearance of traditionalist entities outside the pastoral area of Portuguese colonization, and more specifically in the areas of German and Italian colonization raises an important issue, the fact that the Gaúcho culture, being originally from the Pampas, holds hegemony in a state with incredibly diverse cultural influences, covering not only the cattle areas of the latifundia where the model originated but also the areas of the minifundia in the regions of German and Italian colonization where there never was a pastoral complex. We thus have the first process of *deterritorialization* of Gaúcho culture that leaves its area of origin and is adopted in other regions in Rio Grande do Sul.

Analyzing the meaning of the term *colono* [colonist], Sérgio Alves Teixeira observed that the term has a well-defined historical origin associated with the process of colonization by European immigrants who had as their basis family agriculture and small properties. Since cattle ranching was the dominant activity from the beginning of the Portuguese colonization in the state, it was highly praised, whereas agriculture came to be considered degrading. Thus, from the beginning of the German and Italian colonizations, the term *colono*, besides designating the immigrants and their descendants, "at the symbolic level, it meant, above all, a lack of certain attributes that were considered positive; the term represented a void. *Colono* had the connotation of a person who lacked ambition, social manners, elegance, physical and behavioral posture, a sense of opportunity and progress, fearlessness, perspicacity, and sagacity."[27] Scholars of the colonization point to the fact that foreign immigrants idealized the Gaúcho as a socially superior type. Contributing to this attribute was the fact that the ranchers formed the most powerful social class in the state and that the principal symbol of the Gaúcho was his horse. In Europe the horse was the symbol and mark of distinction of the rural aristocracy. One of the first things the *colonos* did when they arrived in Brazil was to obtain a mount as soon as they could.[28] The identification of the *colono* with the Gaúcho meant, therefore, a symbolic form of upward social mobility. It is interesting that although Rio Grande do Sul may have a large number of German and Italian entrepreneurs and politicians,[29] the "representative" social type remains the Gaúcho.

From 1948 to 1954 thirty-five new traditionalist centers appeared and were distributed practically throughout all the regions in the state, although they were primarily concentrated in the pastoral areas. In the capital a kind of domestic mini-CTG was created.

Around this time, the traditionalists discussed the direction their establishments should take. There were two positions: a more "aristocratic" stance was that there should be a greater preoccupation with the "cultural" level (understood as educated culture) in the CTGs, rejecting the idea that it should only be a place for entertainment; another position thought that it was precisely this aspect—that of entertainment—that was more important and that there should be no prejudice with respect to "popular culture."

In 1954 the distinct centers for tradition that had proliferated since 1948 got together for the first time in a convention that took place in Santa Maria. This meeting was held to discuss the above-mentioned question as well as others. At the meeting a thesis was presented by Luiz Carlos Barbosa Lessa, one of the students who founded the '35 CTG, entitled *The Meaning and Value of Traditionalism*. This was to become the main thesis of the Gaúcho Traditionalist Movement.

The author, twenty-four years old at the time and recently graduated from law school—a career he did not wish to pursue—had come to São Paulo where he enrolled in the School of Sociology and Political Sciences. There he came into contact with the ideas of North American sociologist Donald Pierson, who had graduated from the University of Chicago. Pierson's book, *Theory and Research in Sociology*, as well as the book, *A Study of Man*, written by North American anthropologist Ralph Linton and published in 1936, were both used in the course.[30] Both authors were preoccupied with the effects of population growth, with the consequences of urbanization, and the changes that occurred in the family and the local group, a problematic that recurred in the social sciences at the time. This problematic was heavily influenced by

Durkheim's theories developed in France in the nineteenth century. According to Barbosa Lessa, the course was very boring, and after a few months he returned to Rio Grande do Sul. When he set out to write the major thesis for traditionalism, however, the author realized how close the two North American social scientists were to traditionalist concerns:

> In these two or three months, in 1953, I was given a basic bibliography of books I should acquire, in which *Theory and Research in Sociology* by Donald Pierson and *A Study of Man* by Ralph Linton figured prominently. Then I did not continue the course but returned to Rio Grande do Sul, toward the end of 1953, with at least these two books . . . I went out to the farm in Piratini and I remember that it was there, at the farm, that I read and took notes on these two books and they were a revelation to me. Since I was completely enthralled with traditionalist matters, I started noticing how much these books coincided with what we were doing. It was then that I learned the concept of society, of culture, of tradition, of cultural vision, and so forth. All of those basic concepts. And I realized that I could develop something good. It may seem that at this time, in 1954, I had become engaged in the study of sociology, but I confess, in all sincerity, that I must have read these two books at the time as well as the *Sociology Dictionary* published by Globo Press, which I still consult whenever I need to. This then comprises my entire knowledge of the social sciences in the theoretical realm—these three books and nothing else.[31]

This declaration aptly exemplifies how the knowledge produced by academics becomes common knowledge. In this sense, the Gaúcho Traditionalist Movement is unwittingly one of the greatest disseminators of the ideas of North American social scientists who wrote in the 1940s.

The main thesis of traditionalism began by emphasizing the importance of culture, transmitted by tradition, in order for a society to function as a unit. Every problem resides in the fact that this transmission of culture is not occurring satisfactorily since "culture and Western society are suffering a frightening process of disintegration"; therefore, it is "in the great urban centers that this phenomenon is more clearly sketched out, through ever growing statistics dealing with crime, divorce, suicide, adultery, juvenile delinquency, and other indexes of social disintegration."[32] This social disintegration was the result primarily of two factors: the weakening of the nucleus of local cultures and the gradual disappearance of the "local groups" as units for the transmission of culture.

One can easily recognize in the main thesis of traditionalism described above the influence of nineteenth-century and early-twentieth-century social thought regarding the consequences of urbanization, elaborated indirectly through what the author calls the "masters of modern sociology," namely, members of the Chicago School of Sociology. Although this school is not directly cited, what is described is the phenomenon of *anomie* described by Durkheim as it applies to population growth and the consequent social division of labor. The emphasis on the theme of disintegration and the assertion that the city accelerates this process brings to mind theories of dichotomies and contrast, primarily the theory of the folk-urban continuum by Robert Redfield. This North American anthropologist believed that the consequences of urbanization were the disorganization of culture, secularization, and individualism. City life, he believed, would weaken or destroy the firm bonds that integrated men in a rural society and would create an urban culture characterized by fragmentation of social roles and more secular and individualistic behavior. Homogeneity in a rural society composed of a nonambiguous and monolithic structure would be substituted in urban society by a social structure marked by a diversity of roles, actions, and meanings. Rural culture, within which all cultural elements would be defined, would become a fragmented culture in the urban society. The inevitable consequences of urban culture would then be conflict and disorganization.[33]

How is it that this theory, so fashionable at that time, is still applicable to Rio Grande do Sul and its reality? It is interesting to see how traditionalism provides a "solution" to the social crisis described above:

> [Traditionalism] has as its goal precisely the combating of these two recognized factors of social disintegration. The scientific foundation of this movement can be seen in the following sociological affirmation: "Any society can avoid dissolution while maintaining integrity in its cultural nucleus. The breaking down of this nucleus produces conflicts among the individuals who comprise the society, for they come to prefer different values, resulting in the loss of psychological unity essential to the efficient functioning of any society." Through recreational or sports

activities that characterize the movement—with emphasis always on the traditional motifs of Rio Grande do Sul—traditionalism tries, more than anything, to strengthen the nucleus of Rio Grandian culture, keeping in mind those individuals who stumble aimlessly and without support in our chaotic times. And, through the Centers for Gaúcho Tradition, traditionalism tries to provide the individual with an association that has the same characteristics of the "local group" he lost or fears losing: his homestead. More than his homestead, it is the homestead of generations that preceded him.[34]

Taking a position in the polemic between "cultural qualification" and "popular massification," the main thesis affirms the following:

Traditionalism must be a movement that is clearly *popular*, not simply intellectual. It is true that the ultimate goal of traditionalism will continue to be understood only by an intellectual minority. But in order for the movement to succeed, it is fundamental that it be understood and developed in the bosom of the masses themselves, that is, at the race tracks, the radio halls, the popular festivals and dances, the Festival for the Divine, the Festival for Navigators, and so forth.[35] To achieve its goal, traditionalism must make use of folklore, sociology, art, literature, theater, and so on. All this constitutes the *means* by which traditionalism can achieve its ends. One must not confuse traditionalism, that is, the movement, with folklore, history, sociology, and so forth, which are all sciences. One must not confuse a folklorist, for example, with a traditionalist: the former is a scholar in a scientific pursuit, the latter is a soldier in a movement. Traditionalists do not need to treat folklore scientifically; they will be acting efficiently if they follow, as a basis of their actions, the studies carried out by folklorists, and thus reaffirm the folklore that lives in the bosom of the people themselves.[36]

The option taken in favor of the "popular" tendency implies a division between the masses and the intellectual elite. The members of this latter group can be compared to soldiers whose mission is to formulate the principles and understand the sense of traditionalism, carrying these ideas to the masses who are incapable of understanding the "ultimate goal" of traditionalism, but in whom it must be imbued if the movement wishes to be victorious and strong. In spite of an essentially instrumental vision in relation to sciences and knowledge—seen as a means to achieving the ends of traditionalism, the traditionalist leadership obviously constitutes a group of intellectuals with a sizable number of publications. They can be viewed as intellectuals who are outside the normal circles of academic recognition since they are not affiliated with academic institutions. Interviews carried out with members of this intellectual elite show that if, on the one hand, they try to affirm themselves as intellectuals in Rio Grande do Sul, on the other hand they are viewed with mistrust within their own movement.

> Traditionalism has several wings. There are two main ones: the physiological wing . . . and a cultural cerebral wing that today is very much out of favor, hated by the physiological wing, which has the habit of calling those who study . . . *medalhões* (big shots) . . . We are the big shots of the traditionalist movement. . . . They call us at any moment, bring us together, call us for speeches, but at the time of the conventions, when they see we debate certain issues with them— . . . How does the CTG survive, how does the CTG raise funds, how does it build its headquarters, all of this they can tell you, but don't ask them anything about culture because they will give you nonsensical answers.[37]

The expansion of Traditionalism follows an interesting dynamic. Contrary to the small repercussion the movement might have had in Porto Alegre, in the interior of the state and outside it, its growth was impressive. From the time of the First Traditionalist Congress, which took place in 1954 in Santa Maria, the Centers for Gaúcho Tradition begin meeting annually. In these congresses, theses are presented, motions approved, and deliberations carried out. In the Seventh Traditionalist Congress, which took place in Taquara in 1961, the *Charter of Principles of the Traditionalist Movement* was approved. This document was written by Glaucus Saraiva, one of the founders of the '35 CTG. He is also the author of the *Traditionalist Manual*, published in 1968, which offers orientation for traditionalists and for the Centers for Gaúcho Traditions.[38] During the Twelfth Traditionalist Congress, which took place in Tramandaí in 1966, the Gaúcho Traditionalist Movement was founded and included the majority of the traditionalist entities in the state. The GTM is the "catalyst, disciplinarian, and guide of the activities of its affiliates in matters established in the *Charter of Principles of the Traditionalist Movement.*"[39] All these institutions are ruled by that charter.

Traditionalism was also expanded in other directions. Thus, in 1954, the state government created, within the Division of Culture of the Department of Education and Culture, the Institute of Traditions and Folklore. In 1974 the latter was transformed into the Foundation Gaúcho Institute of Tradition and Folklore, an organ normally led by traditionalists named to leadership positions. In 1964 a state law was approved giving official status to Farroupilha Week, which was to be commemorated annually from September 14 to September 20. This provided for the "Creole Flame" to receive all the honors of Piratini Palace, the headquarters of the state government. Moreover, this law made official the parade that takes place every year on September 20 with representatives of the Centers for Gaúcho Tradition and the Military Brigade in almost every city in the state. In 1966 another state law made official the Farroupilha Anthem as the anthem for Rio Grande do Sul. During the Triches government (1971–75), in Palacio Piratini, a Creole bunkhouse was created in an attempt to re-create the ranch environment, where receptions with Rio Grandian barbecues and the typical dish *carreteiro*[40] were held and presentations of dances and Rio Grandian music were staged for famous visitors to the state. In this same period the state donated land to enable the " '35 CTG" to build its own headquarters. In 1979 the Department of Culture, Sports, and Tourism was created. This move meant the untangling of cultural matters from the Department of Education and Culture. The second person to occupy the new office was Luiz Carlos Barbosa Lessa, one of the founders of the '35 CTG. The new director created cultural poles that cemented the fact that twelve cultural regions existed in the state. These poles were established to disseminate cultural ideas into the interior of the state.[41] This created an incentive toward regionalist activities that began to gain an importance through support that they had not had before.[42] In 1988 a state law was approved to establish within the teaching of social studies the study of folklore in all the state's elementary and secondary schools. In 1989 a state law made official the *pilchas* (the typical suit of the old Gaúcho, made up of the *bombacha* [baggy Gaúcho pants], boots, bandanna, and hat) as the "honor suit and to be of preferential use" in the state, leaving its characterization to the "dicta and directions of the Gaúcho Traditionalist Movement."

As far as civil society was concerned, traditionalism was also able to irradiate the cult to Gaúcho traditions. Thus the Ranch of Creole Poetry was created. It is a kind of academy of letters for writers of Gaúcho themes. As for the Church, one need only point out the appearance of the Creole mass with a liturgy inspired by the Gaúcho thematic in which God is called the "Celestial Boss," the Virgin Mary is the "First Maiden of the Heavens," and Saint Peter is the "Foreman of the Gaúcho Ranch." Similarly, the Creole wedding, in which the bride and groom are dressed according to tradition, is also quite common in the state. In several cities in the interior, there are festive roundups where field struggles are relived. The GTM annually promotes a pageant where the First Maiden is chosen. In 1971, in Uruguaiana, a city located in the area of the *Campanha*, on the initiative of the Center for Gaúcho Traditions, *Sinuelo do Pago*, the California[43] of Gaúcho native songs, the first festival of native state music, took place. This festival, which takes place annually, serves as the model for some forty festivals that exist in the state today and that are spread throughout its most diverse regions. These events normally bring together thousands of young people who generally camp out, evoking in their environment the country life and symbols of a regional Gaúcho identity.[44]

Although the GTM is not able to control all the state's cultural expressions,[45] clearly the traditionalist movement has experienced significant numerical growth in the number of participants as well as in its sphere of influence, to the point where today it is considered by its leaders to be "the largest popular culture movement in the Western world," which, according to them, has "the direct participation of two million people."[46]

The data regarding the number of Centers for Gaúcho Tradition are quite precarious and must be taken with due care. Writing in 1976, a historian of Traditionalism affirmed that "after a mere three decades, around 600 traditionalist entities were created. Of these, some 400 are still operational and have traditionalism as their sole reason for existing."[47] Again in 1979, the number of 400 CTGs was mentioned in the introduction to the new edition of *Meaning and Value of Traditionalism*.[48] However, at some point, the number of CTGs mentioned by the local press grew and varied considerably and, in general, did not correspond to the actual data. A newspaper report in 1986 referred to the existence of 1,000 CTGs in the state, and in 1989 another spoke of "almost 1,500 Centers for Gaúcho Traditions,"[49] whereas data reported by the GTM itself in 1987 indicated there were 886 traditionalist entities, including the CTGs, the *piquetes* (small groups of horsemen), and so on. In a more recent statement, the vice president of GTM indicated that there were 1,196 CTGs affiliated with the Gaúcho Traditionalist Movement in 1988.[50] According to a GTM member, this group would include not only the CTGs, but all traditionalist entities found in the state, including the small groups of horsemen, folklore groups, as well as other associations, since practically all of them are affiliated with the Movement. In 1994 it was estimated that 1,320 CTGs existed in Rio Grande do Sul.[51] It is relatively simple to form a CTG, and one is frequently created after internal strife within an existing group; hence the large number of this and other types of traditionalist entities in small cities. In the words of an ex-boss of a CTG:

> The citizen who is frustrated with community life, who cannot rise socially in society or in the Rotary Club, the Lions Club, or in Masonry, could easily enter the CTG. This individual decides to found a CTG, does so with the greatest of ease, and then becomes a leader. Then he appears in the media, is interviewed, gains relevance in the community. This explains the large number of CTGs in the state. . . . The moment he is defeated by an adversary faction in the CTG, he simply cannot take the defeat . . . and, in order to separate himself, begins . . . another CTG.[52]

At this point, we must differentiate between the CTGs and the *piquetes*, or small groups of horsemen mentioned above. According to members of the Gaúcho Traditionalist Movement, the difference between the two types of associations is that whereas the CTGs are more "complete" entities, the *piquetes* are merely "parts" of a whole; that is, a Center for Gaúcho Traditions functions as a kind of club (in fact the only club in several localities), comprising several "departments" that are called *invernadas* (the name evokes the great land areas that are fenced off in the ranches and used for fattening cattle). A CTG is characterized by the many activities it executes in the social area (for example, parties and *fandangos*, or dances), in the cultural area (music and recitals), and in the fields (rodeos and wild horseback riding). The CTG has headquarters that also function as a center of entertainment and pleasure. The *piquete* (the name evokes the small stables beside the house where domestic animals are placed daily for grazing; the name also reminds us of peons who at every moment are occupied by farm services) would be one of these "departments" of the CTGs, since it dedicates itself only to field activities, leaving aside those of a cultural or social nature as more appropriate to the CTGs. The *piquete* does not need headquarters and can have a smaller number of members. Ideally, a *piquete* should be affiliated with a CTG, but this is not always the case. Ultimately, the Gaúcho Traditionalist Movement, facing the creation of a large number of *piquetes*, ended up registering them as autonomous entities rather than as part of the CTGs. The *piquetes* apparently arose because of the divergence in the groups belonging to a single CTG; when a particular group became dissatisfied with the "politics" adopted by the CTG, they created their own field department and called it a *piquete*.[53] Since these groups are composed of a smaller number of members and do not need headquarters in order to become affiliated with the Gaúcho Traditionalism Movement, this type of association spread throughout the state. It should be pointed out, however, that this expansion may also indicate a preference for "field" activities among the traditionalists.

Despite the discrepancy in data and their possible exaggeration, clearly there was an accentuated growth in the number of traditionalist entities in the last few years. It is worthwhile to examine their distribution in the different regions of the state.

The Gaúcho Traditionalism Movement divides Rio Grande do Sul, from a strictly administrative point of view, into twenty-seven regions. Although the criteria for determining the regions are principally geographical, members of the movement admit that the criteria do vary and that today another type of injunction is always present. In the words of one of the members: "In the beginning the regional divisions were the result of geographical location and, until recently, traditionalist regions corresponded to educational regions in the state. . . . However, today we know that there is always a political question in the background" (see Map 2).

We will not examine the twenty-seven traditionalist regions established by the Gaúcho Traditionalist Movement but will look

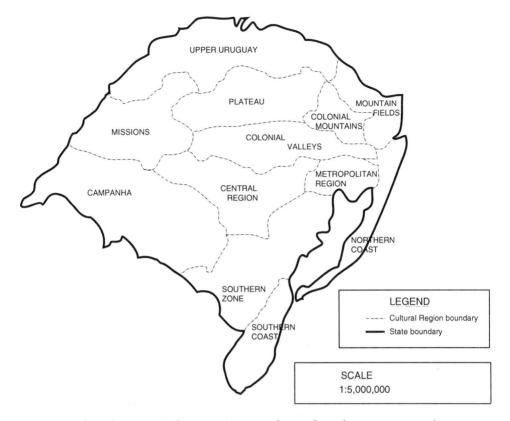

instead at the state's division into twelve cultural regions, or cultural poles, established by the then director of the Department of Culture, Sports, and Tourism, Barbosa Lessa. The objective of this division was to bring about a cultural map of the state, in an attempt to learn about and give value to the cultural aspects of the different municipalities in the state. Besides the geographical aspects, it obeys criteria that take into consideration historical, ethnic, cultural, and other characteristics in each region. The twelve regions are as follows: Northern Coast, Missions, Mountain Fields, Southern Coast, Central Region, Southern Zone, *Campanha*, Colonial Valleys, Colonial Mountains, Plateau Region, Upper Uruguay, and Metropolitan Region.

If we compare the 1987 data of the Gaúcho Traditionalist Movement regarding the traditionalist entities to the population data reported in the same year by the Brazilian Institute of Geography and Statistics about the municipalities that integrate the cultural regions, we are able to determine the distribution of traditionalist regions in the state (Table 1).

Table 1
DISTRIBUTION OF TRADITIONALIST ENTITIES THROUGHOUT THE
CULTURAL REGIONS OF RIO GRANDE DO SUL

Region	CTGs	Others	Total	Population	Pop./CTG	Pop./Total
Northern Coast	23	26	49	174,969	7,607	3,570
Missions	26	10	36	373,134	14,351	10,365
Mountain Fields	21	37	58	157,556	7,503	2,716
Southern Coast	12	1	13	218,855	18,238	16,835
Central Region	77	61	138	644,719	8,373	4,672
Southern Zone	34	18	52	516,062	15,178	9,924
Campanha	62	28	90	607,909	9,805	6,755
Colonial Valleys	63	17	80	1,161,610	18,438	14,520
Colonial Mountains	41	30	71	560,697	13,676	7,897
Plateau Region	53	84	137	729,536	13,765	5,325
Upper Uruguay	71	11	82	871,182	12,270	10,624
Metropolitan Region	59	21	80	2,124,549	36,009	26,557
Total	542	344	886	8,140,778	15,020	9,188

The regions that present the greatest proportion of traditionalist entities in relation to the population are, in order of magnitude, the Mountain Fields, the Northern Coast, and the Central Region. It is also in these regions where we find a greater number of *piquetes* than CTGs. One characteristic of these regions is that they are generally composed of small municipalities, that is, municipalities with populations between four thousand and twenty thousand, as well as some cities with average populations, such as Vacaria, Cachoeira do Sul, and Santa Maria. Another characteristic is the relative proximity of these regions to Porto Alegre within the context of the state. These data place in doubt the current idea that Traditionalism would be stronger in the border region. One could argue that in those regions, country life is part and parcel of daily life, and thus it need not be re-created.

The regions with the smallest proportion of traditionalist entities in relation to population are, also in order of magnitude, the Metropolitan Region, the Colonial Valleys, and the Southern Coast. Although each of these three regions has specific characteristics, a common trait among them is the presence of municipalities with large populations. The Metropolitan Region of Porto Alegre is made up completely of cities with great population densities, the smallest having approximately sixty thousand people. The Southern Coastal Region has a city of average size, which is

the city of Rio Grande. In the Colonial Valley, there are some aver-
age-sized municipalities, such as Novo Hamburgo, São Leopoldo,
and Santa Cruz do Sul. The first two are legally part of greater Porto
Alegre, but they are included in that cultural region since they are
of German colonization.

These data suggest that an inverse relationship exists between
the population of a municipality and the proportion of traditionalist entities in that city. This may be linked, among other elements,
to the fact that in the larger and more urbanized municipalities,
besides rural activities not predominating, other forms of pleasure
and recreation are available, such as movies, theaters, bars, shows,
and so on. Of course this relationship is not direct or unequivocal,
since each municipality has its own peculiarities.

It can be argued that a CTG, besides having the regionalist aspect,
functions as a kind of club where the "members" pay a monthly fee,
which, as members of the Gaúcho Traditionalist Movement point
out, is always less expensive than that of any other club. This being
so, the traditionalist entities enable a greater number of people to
participate. However, although the monthly fees may be small, to
participate fully in the activities of a CTG, such as in the dances,
rodeos, parties, and so on, the member needs at the very least to be
donned in the typical costume (boots, bombachas [baggy Gaúcho
pants], hat, traditional flowery dress, and so on.) In addition, certain
activities require that participants invest quite a lot of money, such
as in field activities when a horse is needed or when a member must
travel to another municipality to participate in rodeos.

The expansion of traditionalism goes beyond Rio Grande do Sul,
one of the states with the largest emigration rates in Brazil. From
1920 to 1950 the Gaúcho exodus comprised 300,000 people. In this
last year, Rio Grande do Sul was the state that furnished the
largest emigration contingent to other states, although it
remained the unit in the federation that received the smallest
number of other Brazilians. This emigration generally comes from
the interior of Rio Grande do Sul to the interior of other states,
people in search of new agricultural frontiers, mainly in the states
of Santa Catarina, Paraná, and Mato Grosso. For a breakdown of
the number of Gaúchos in other states in the Southern Region, see
Table 2.

Table 2
NUMBER OF GAÚCHOS IN OTHER STATES IN THE SOUTHERN REGION
(In thousands of people)

Year	Santa Catarina	Paraná
1940	75	15
1950	120	35
1960	200	160
1970	260	340
1980	300	385

In 1980 there were approximately 900,000 Gaúchos living outside of Rio Grande do Sul, which is some 11.5 percent of the state's
population. More than 50,000 of them had established in Mato
Grosso, indicating a new form of agricultural expansion.[54]

Faced with this impressive Diaspora, it is not surprising that in
1994, in Santa Catarina, there were 245 CTGs[55] and more than 200
piquetes distributed in 93 of its 199 municipalities. It is significant
that the first CTGs were created in 1959 in São Miguel do Oeste in
the extreme western region of Santa Catarina, and, in 1961, in
Lages, located in the southeastern region of this state, both strong
areas of Gaúcho expansion. In 1962 the Traditionalist Movement
of Santa Catarina was created. Later it was called the Gaúcho
Traditionalist Association, and in the 1980s it became the Gaúcho
Traditionalist Movement of Santa Catarina. However, the dissemination of Centers for Gaúcho Tradition in Santa Catarina "is not
just happening in those regions where the migratory flux of Rio
Grandians was intense in the nineteenth and early twentieth centuries, . . . but also on the Coast (Portuguese and Azorians) and in
the Slopes (German, Austrian, Italian, and so on), areas that when
formed did not have any Gaúcho influence."[56]

In the state of Paraná, there are 242 CTGs affiliated with the
Gaúcho Traditionalist Movement of Paraná, which is divided into
thirteen regions. Several members of these CTGs are descendants of
Japanese immigrants who arrived in São Paulo at the beginning of
the century. "Gauchism" is such a strong movement in Paraná that
an issue of the journal of the Cultural Foundation of Curitiba was
entirely dedicated to this question. The author of the text, suggestively entitled "Pass the Gourd, Chê!" [Pass the traditional tea,

partner!], states that "CTGs should not be seen as belonging exclusively to Rio Grande do Sul. . . . The Centers for Gaúcho Tradition relive traditional customs that are common to Uruguay, Argentina, Rio Grande do Sul, Santa Catarina, and Paraná. We are all 'Gaúchos' or in reality Gaúcho, old acquaintances, drinkers of *mate* tea, and consumers of barbecue."[57] And in Mato Grosso do Sul, there are approximately thirty-five CTGs affiliated with the Federation of Lasso Clubs. In São Paulo, the most populated state in Brazil, approximately forty CTGs exist today. Centers for Gaúcho Tradition also exist in several other states in Brazil. The recently created Gaúcho Traditionalist Union of the Northeast comprises seven CTGs. In October 1988 the First Brazilian Congress on Gaúcho Tradition was held in Santa Catarina. The Congress took the first steps toward creating the present-day Brazilian Federation of Gaúcho Tradition.[58] The adoption of tradition that originates in the *Campanha* by inhabitants from other areas in Rio Grande do Sul meant the first steps toward *deterritorialization* of Gaúcho culture that left its point of origin and acquired new meanings and new contexts. The maintenance of Gaúcho culture on the part of Rio Grandians who migrated to other states also represents a new process of *deterritorialization*, which is important because Gaúcho culture continues with their descendants who often have never been in Rio Grande do Sul.

It may be argued that the German and Italian colonists who emigrated from Rio Grande do Sul to establish themselves in other units of Brazil, on creating a cult of customs and values from the ranches in the *Campanha*, are identifying with a world to which they never really belonged. When they left the state, where they were at best the proprietors of a few acres of land and acquired a much larger land area in the region of the agricultural frontiers, they symbolically stopped being small *colonos* and transformed themselves into great ranchers, that is, Gaúchos. A third process of *deterritorialization* is taking place with the Rio Grandians who are migrating abroad. This occurs not only with those who go to cultivate lands in neighboring countries such as Paraguay, but also with those who go to First-World countries. It is estimated that today there are half a million Brazilians living in the United States, Europe, and Japan. And where there are Rio Grandians, there are also CTGs. In 1992 a CTG was created in Los Angeles and another in

Osaka, Japan. The latter has the name "CTG of the Rising Sun," proving that cultures travel with their carriers and take hold in other soils.[59]

It is not beyond the realm of imagination that in the future more CTGs will exist outside than inside Rio Grande do Sul. Even though this large number of traditionalist entities in other states and countries probably will no longer be frequented by native Gaúchos but by their descendants, the existence of these CTGs denotes an immense wistfulness and longing for the old homestead and a search for lost rural origins (or perhaps origins one never had) in a manner similar to what happened to the founders of the '35 CTG.[60]

7. Gaúcho in the *Campanha* region (bordering Argentina).
Courtesy of Luiz Eduardo Achutti

8. Gaúchos in a small bar in the *Campanha* region.
Courtesy of Luiz Eduardo Achutti

9. A traditionalist musician who lives in the state's capital, Porto Alegre, drinking *mate* tea at the California of Rio Grande do Sul Native Song Festival that takes place annually in Uruguaiana in the *Campanha* region. The shirt is from the International Sport Club, one of the best-known soccer teams in Rio Grande do Sul—at the time the team was sponsored by Coca-Cola. Courtesy of Luiz Eduardo Achutti

10. A couple of tourists from São Paulo visiting the California of Rio Grande do Sul Native Song Festival. The man, of Japanese ancestry, is dressed like a Gaúcho. Courtesy of Luiz Eduardo Achutti

11. Camp in the California of Rio Grande do Sul Native Song Festival.
Courtesy of Luiz Eduardo Achutti

12. Stage for the presentation of the California of Rio Grande do Sul Native Song, featuring some musicians performing.
Courtesy of Luiz Eduardo Achutti

13. A student of Gaúcho music playing the accordion in a show in Porto Alegre. Courtesy of Luiz Eduardo Achutti

14. A young man performing a Gaúcho dance in a traditional barbecue restaurant in Porto Alegre. Courtesy of Luiz Eduardo Achutti

Chapter Five

THE SOCIAL CONSTRUCTION OF THE GAÚCHO IDENTITY

●

In an effort to present a cultural overview of the 1970s in Rio Grande do Sul, a journalist published an article entitled "Regionalism Does Not Resist the Invasion of Discotheques" in which he affirmed that the state "has been invaded during the 1970s by mass culture. Never, in any other time in our history, has the Piratini territory been so much at the mercy of sophisticated invaders. They came in slowly, without hurry or fear, first in black and white and later in color. Our culture, impotent to resist, began to assimilate strange habits, and regionalism was hung out to dry in the back like a *guaiaca*"[1] [a wide belt with many small pockets used by Gaúchos to store weapons, money, and other objects].

However, when one observes the cultural manifestations that were evident during the 1980s and 1990s, the number of activities linked to traditions is impressive. The revival of Gaúcho memorabilia is responsible for approximately a thousand traditionalist entities, more than forty Gaúcho music festivals involving a population of approximately a million people,[2] and several rodeos. This growing interest also helps to explain the consumption of cultural products surrounding Gaúcho themes: television and radio programs (there is even an FM radio station in the metropolitan region of Porto Alegre that plays Gaúcho music exclusively, defining itself as a "*bombacha*-wearing radio station"[3]), newspaper columns, magazines and specialized newspapers, publishing houses, books, bookstores, and regional book fairs, publicity that refers directly to Gaúcho values,[4] folk dance halls,[5] music groups, singers and records, typical restaurants featuring music and dance shows, stores that specialize in Gaúcho clothing, and so on. It all adds up to a significant market for material and symbolic goods that moves a great number of people and resources and that seems to be expanding.

Although there always was consumer demand for Gaúcho cultural products, it was much smaller and was concentrated in the countryside or in the suburban and urban layers of society that had rural origins. The novelty is that young people in the cities, a good number of them from the middle class, have recently begun to drink *chimarrão*, to wear *bombachas*, and to enjoy regional music—all habits that have lost their stigma of inferiority. Considering that more than 75 percent of the state's population lives in urban settings, this market is concentrated in the cities and is formed, for the most part, by people who have had no experience living in rural areas.[6]

The image that readily emerges when one hears of Gaúcho things is based on a past that existed in the pastoral region of the *Campanha* in the southwest of Rio Grande do Sul and on the real or idealized figure of the Gaúcho. This is the center around which the debates about Gaúcho identity turn. Today, the construction of this representation posits the question in a new light since we are in an era during which Rio Grande do Sul has become urbanized and modern. At the same time, Brazil itself has developed a greater integration in politics, economics, transportation, communication, and so on, articulating its regions in an effective way.

Such a construction of identity excludes more than it includes, leaving out half the Rio Grandian territory and a large part of its social groups. In spite of the weakening of the southern region of the state, in spite of the notable economic and political projection of the descendants of the German and Italian colonists who developed the northern region, and in spite of the urbanization and industrialization in the state, the representative figure in Rio

Grande do Sul continues to be the Gaúcho from the *Campanha* as it was in the past.

If the construction of this identity tends to exalt the Gaúcho to the detriment of those colonists of German and Italian descent, then it excludes to an even greater extent the blacks and the Indians who, if represented at all, are only included in an extremely faint way.

When one analyzes data with respect to skin color in the Brazilian demographic census of 1980, one finds that Rio Grande do Sul is the second "whitest" state in Brazil, with 87.16 percent of the population declaring itself white, 8.14 percent brown, and 4.21 percent black. These data are in contrast to those of Brazil which show that only 54.23 percent of the population declares itself white, 38.85 percent declares itself brown, and 5.92 percent declares itself black.[7]

The question, however, centers less on self-classification of skin color as on the social and symbolic invisibility of blacks in Rio Grande do Sul. Analyzing racial ideologies and their influence in the construction of national identity in Brazil, Renato Ortiz showed that at the end of the nineteenth century, one begins to see the formation of a melting pot ideology in Brazil. At that time Brazilian literature had *O Guarani* by José de Alencar, which constructed an idealized Indian. At the turn of the century, there appeared the myth of the three races that form the Brazilian nationality, today considered common knowledge but then considered news, namely, that Brazil is the result of the hybridity of the three races. In the 1930s, Gilberto Freyre

> transformed the negativity of the hybrid into positivity, thus bringing about the definite completion of the outlines of an identity that was being drawn for a long time. Except that social conditions now were different. Brazilian society was no longer in a period of transition; the paths of development were clear and even a new state tried to guide these changes. The myth of the three races became plausible then and could come to be ritualized. The ideology of the hybrid that was imprisoned in the ambiguities of racist theories, became reelaborated and could be disseminated through social channels and become common knowledge that was ritually celebrated in day-to-day relationships or in such great events as Carnival or soccer. What was hybrid became national.[8]

While examining northeastern regionalism, Beatriz Góis Dantas demonstrated that in 1930, the exaltation of black culture was used in the creation of a national culture. This construction came in the wake of the modernist movements that tried to cut ties with Europe and discover Brazilian originality through the valorizing of cultural traits that had originated in Africa. Specifically in the case of northeastern regionalism, the role of the black was emphasized positively: "This way, if the exaltation of black culture was used to create a national culture, the glorification of the African, more specifically of the *nagô* [referring to the people of S. E. Daome in Africa] would serve to mark regional differences, for it was in the Northeast, and particularly in the state of Bahia, that Africanisms were believed to have been preserved more closely."[9]

However, just as in other states in Brazil, like the state of Bahia, blacks played a role in forming the national identity, in Rio Grande do Sul their image was relegated to a secondary level. In fact, traditional Gaúcho historiography, in spite of recognizing the generalized existence of slaves in the state, insisted on their limited importance in the labor process.

In Gaúcho folklore, the most salient presence of the black is in the legend of the *Negrinho do Pastoreio* [Little Black Boy Who Tended the Pasture]. The legend has several versions, the most famous one written by the great regionalist author Simões Lopes Neto. It is the story of a slave boy who lost a horse race on which his owner had bet a great sum of money. As a punishment, after he was beaten, he had to tend the pasture of a small herd of horses that ended up getting away. This brought about another beating and the demand that he find the runaway horses. To carry out his task, the Little Black Boy thought about the Virgin Mary and took a candle that dripped all along the way. Each of the drops lit up so that the entire field was illuminated, thus making it possible for the Little Black Boy to find the herd. But the rancher's son, who was evil, let the horses go, and once again the slave was beaten. This time he appeared to be dead and was left on top of an ant hill to be eaten. To the astonishment of the rancher, three days later the Little Black Boy was found in perfect health; beside him was the herd of horses and the Virgin. Therefore, today the "Little Black Boy always looks for lost objects, placing them so that their owners will find them when they light a candle which the Little Black Boy takes to the altar of Our Lady the Virgin, Godmother to all who do not have one."[10]

This narrative, which involves death, resurrection, and popular beatification, unfolds in the pastoral environment of a ranch in which the ideology of southern racial democracy projected a harmonious life without any suffering for the slave. Although at the end of the legend one finds the ascension of the Little Black Boy, he still continues to serve others, looking for things they lost. It is interesting that an author who wrote an important critical analysis about this legend, comparing it to other Brazilian legends (such as that of the Saci, a one-legged little black boy who smokes a pipe and wears a red beret and has magical powers), would insist that the Gaúcho legend did not have "any Afro-Brazilian basis, but only formal elements of African origin. Its meaning is very Christian, in spite of a certain accidental mixture of paganism."[11]

Even today, when one speaks of Rio Grande do Sul, one seldom mentions the presence of blacks and black culture. This is surprising when we consider that the state in general and its capital in particular have an impressive activity in *Umbanda* (Brazilian religion that combines elements from African religions, Roman Catholicism, and elements related to Alan Kardec's Spiritism) and *Batuque* (the name given to African religions in Rio Grande do Sul and the generic name for the music of percussion instruments, usually associated with black culture).

The French sociologist Roger Bastide, who was in Porto Alegre in 1944, verified, while working with the files of the capital's police department, that there was an impressive growth of cult establishments, from thirteen in 1937 to fifty-seven in 1942. In his research of the files of the four Afro-Brazilian religious federations that exist today in the state, Ari Pedro Oro calculates that at the end of the 1980s, there were approximately 2,500 cult establishments in Porto Alegre, 4,000 in the other cities of the metropolitan region surrounding the state capital, and 5,800 in the interior of the state, bringing the total to 11,800 throughout the state. In reality, the numbers were much higher since many centers were not registered.[12] Oro points to the existence of a small but significant number of Italian and German descendants who participate in these religions either as believers or as spiritual leaders: "4.1 percent of the total number of Afro-Brazilian religious centers in Rio Grande do Sul are in the hands of individuals of Italian and German origin. This percentage is 6.5 percent for Porto Alegre, 3.5 percent for the greater Porto Alegre, and 3.3 percent for the interior of the state."

The author presents, as one of the hypotheses of the phenomenon, the idea that,

> the participation of the Italian and German descendants of Rio Grande do Sul in Afro-Brazilian religions deepens their integration into Brazilian society inasmuch as one observes a significant decrease in social relations with their Italian and German compatriots who are Catholic or Protestant, as well as a deepening of relations with individuals of Afro-Brazilian origin. This phenomenon at the same time configures a possible "blackening" in the way of being and thinking of these descendants of European immigrants, and is a further sign of their "Brazilianizing."[13]

With regard to the Indians, inasmuch as their number in the state has been so greatly reduced (comprising 0.1 percent of the population), it is possible to appropriate their symbols and transform them into symbols of regional identity. Thus, in one of the versions of the Rio Grandian identity, it is considered a source of pride that the Gaúcho has Indian blood. It is common to use the expression "old Indian," as a term of endearment, referring to the figure of the Gaúcho. Contributing to this idea are the following factors: the Indians were so reduced in number that they therefore had little contact with whites; the Indians were not enslaved at the same rate as the blacks; the image of the Indian is one of courage and pride; and the *charruas* and *minuanos*, groups that no longer exist but that inhabited the *Campanha* when the Iberians arrived, were warriors, and after the introduction of the horse, they became expert horsemen, models for the brave and proud figure of the Gaúcho who is permanently in contact with and struggle with nature. In this last case, the connection is made via the horse, an emblematic element of the Gaúcho.[14]

What one sees nowadays, however, are the descendants of the *Guarani* and of the *Kaingang*, indigenous groups that still remain in the state, trying to defend themselves against the landless white peasants who try to appropriate the Indian lands. This situation does not stop Rio Grande do Sul from proclaiming, as a symbol of Gaúcho bravery, the figure of Sepé Tiaraju, a leader of the *Guarani* who opposed the surrendering of their land in the Missions region to the white man during the eighteenth century. The war cry "this land has an owner," which has been attributed to him, is often used today as a protest against any external intervention in state matters.

It is interesting to note that although blacks and Indians are repressed in the state, both ethnic groups are represented symbolically in *Carnival*, a rite of passage characterized precisely by inversion. It is significant that Pelotas, considered to be the most aristocratic of all Gaúcho cities and located in an area where beef jerky processing plants were abundant, featured a Black *Rei Momo* (king of the Carnival festivities) a few years ago. Likewise, in Porto Alegre, some of the groups that participate in the Carnival merrymaking are called "tribes." The involvement of blacks in the capital's Carnival celebration is significant, with several Samba Schools [organized groups of dancers and musicians that from the 1930s have participated in Carnival parades in large cities] linked to traditional black groups. However, this festivity does not receive the same importance it has, for example, in Rio de Janeiro, in Salvador (capital of the state of Bahia), or in Recife or Olinda (cities in the northeastern state of Pernambuco). Some years ago, an incident occurred that emphasized the ethnic attention that Carnival arouses. The princess of the Porto Alegre Carnival in 1989, a green-eyed blonde, resigned a few days after receiving the title, alleging she was suffering racial discrimination from blacks because she was a blonde.[15] In fact, a series of ethnic incidents punctuate the history of that city. The Grêmio Futebol Porto-Alegrense, one of the most traditional soccer teams, was considered racist because, in its first years of existence, it did not accept black players. Its anthem, however, was composed by Lupicínio Rodrigues, the great black musician who himself was the victim of racial discrimination from the International Sport Club, another traditional team, more popular and "more black" as their mascot was the figure of the Saci.[16] In 1984 Daisy Nunes, a mulatto woman, after one club refused to allow her to be a candidate, won the pageant of Swimming Pool Queen, sponsored by the International Sport Club. In 1986 she was chosen Miss Rio Grande do Sul and later became Miss Brazil, becoming the first woman of color to receive these titles. This has been interpreted by some as proof that no racism exists in the state or in Brazil and by others as proof that the value of beauty pageants has deteriorated.

In 1982 Alceu Collares, a black politician, ran for governor of the state and came in third. Although he won in the capital, he lost to two other candidates in the interior. This was interpreted at the time as a refusal of the electorate in the areas of German and Italian colonization to vote for a black candidate. In 1985 Collares was elected mayor of Porto Alegre. In 1990 he once again became a candidate for governor and came in first in practically all Rio Grandian regions.

The fieldwork I conducted in 1984 at the Second South American Native Music Festival revealed interesting information with respect to the construction of the Gaúcho identity. This festival came into being in 1983 with the purpose of motivating new musical tendencies, since the majority of other festivals in the state did not admit compositions that were dissonant with patterns considered to be nativist music. Santa Rosa, the headquarters city for this festival, is located in the northwestern portion of the state in the Missions region, at the border with the Argentine Missions region, As the name indicates, it was the territory where the Guarani Indians were brought together by the Jesuits until their expulsion from Brazil in the eighteenth century. Later, the region received an influx of colonists who were descendants of the German and Italian immigrants. It is a city where one sees many blonds, such as the popular TV personality, Xuxa, who incidentally is from the area. During my stay in Santa Rosa, I saw only one black person. I stayed at the festival camp along with a large number of young people, who spent their days drinking *chimarrão*, chatting, listening to music, singing, and attending the free shows. They were all white. But what surprised me was that, with great frequency, they sang songs that spoke of their Guarani blood. . . . I looked in vain for Indians in the camp and in the city. At night, there were presentations of competing musical compositions, an event that took place in a movie theater downtown and was attended largely by the local population. As a professor I was interviewed by a newspaper covering the festival, and I stated that, nowadays, in Brazil, one cannot be Brazilian without being regional first. My comment, believed to be the word of the university, was repeated as a legitimizing factor for the festival.

The majority of the musical compositions dealt with the Gaúcho, exalting or trying to de-ideologize his figure. One of the competing songs was dissonant, however, from the tone of the event, innovative not only in its content but in its melody and arrangement. It was the composition "Brazilian Song Number 3" by Maria Rita Stumpf, which spoke of the Kamaiurá Indians from Amazonia and of the Kaingang Indians from Rio Grande do Sul. The rhythm of this composition attempted to reproduce the indigenous music ("Kamayurá in Xingu wants to speak / Kamayurá in Xingu wants land / Kaingang in Nonoai wants land / Kaigangmayurá Kaigangmayurá"). In a festival that purports to be "open" and nativist, there was no way to disqualify or ignore this composition, which, instead of speaking to the traditional state figure, brought forth the matter of the Indians. After long deliberation, the jury ended up awarding it third place.

I wrote in my field diary:

> If I were asked what people celebrate, I would say that they celebrate themselves, individually, in groups, or while they participate in a festival. The people seem to enjoy everything: the heat, the sounds, the mosquitoes, the filth, the show by Mercedes Sosa (in a way the spotlight of the celebration), the *fandangos* (popular dances), the *mate* tea, and so on . . . The thrill is intense in the auditorium and what attracts my attention is that the public indiscriminately applauds the music whether it is in favor of or against the traditional figure of the Gaúcho. In fact, in spite of the festival's self-declared innovative character, one finds compositions ranging from the very traditional to the highly innovative. But the public seems thrilled with all of them; I think that, in reality, people are thrilled with the celebration of Gaúcho identity. There is a sea of blond heads, many of them who probably consider themselves heirs of the Guarani Indians of the Seven Peoples of the Missions, affirming that they have something different from the rest of Brazilians. In fact, one does not speak of Samba, Carnival, or *candomblé* [name given to African religions in the state of Bahia] but of mate tea, warriors, Indians, Gaúchos, cattle, pestle, and so on.

The music festival usually invites a well-known artist to be a guest star on one of the nights of the festival to show the festival's open spirit. That year Mercedes Sosa was invited. Sosa, besides originating from Argentina, the country that borders the Missions region, is a symbol of Latin American identity. On the night of her presentation, she sang from a stage that had been set up in a soccer stadium filled with an estimated ten thousand people, despite the drizzling rain. The artist enchanted her public with her songs, which emphasized the "Latin soul" of their America. Young people joined her in song, and one young man was even successful in evading the guards and jumping onto the stage where, in tears, he embraced the singer, emotionally affecting the entire audience. When the show came to an end, the rain was pouring down in buckets. It was the time that marked the end of the military regime and the start of the campaign for "Direct elections now!" (*Diretas já!*), and when Mercedes Sosa finished her show, the public spontaneously began shouting the phrase, "One, two, three four, five thousand [*mil*], we want to elect the president of Brazil!"

Analyzing the symbology of the event, I was able to establish that it was a festival of identities: Missioneiro identity [referring to the Jesuit missions and the current cultural tradition of the region], Guarani-Kaingang identity, Gaúcho identity, Latin American identity, and, finally, thanks to the presidential elections, Brazilian identity—all this to indicate that to arrive at a Brazilian identity, it was necessary to follow a very winding path.

Thales de Azevedo, reflecting on the revival of Gauchism, ponders the following:

[This phenomenon] seems to evidence a desire for affirmation of Gaúcho identity and for national identity; at the same time, however, perhaps it is a desire to affirm the differences—quite apparent in several aspects—of the Gaúcho culture compared to Brazilians from other areas, particularly those from Luso-African traditions and culture, now so visible in folklore, music, and so on, particularly with the salience that television gives to such traits. The Gaúchos, who are now returning to their *bombacha* pants, to *chimarrão*, to *chimarrita* (a historic popular dance and poetry accompanied by viola or guitar), seem to identify themselves as "whiter" and even more linked to their Prata region neighbors than to mulatto and black Brazilians from the North of the country or to the hybrid from Amazonia or from the Northeast. They also want to assimilate the immigrants (Italians, Germans, etc.).[17]

During the 1980s Gaúcho identity was the object of an intense and heated debate. Although trying to position themselves in opposite camps, in their hearts both contenders were revolving around the same semantic field: the figure of the Gaúcho, the means of constructing it, the criteria for defining its authenticity, the instances of its legitimacy and consecration, and so on.

Basically two types of contenders were involved in this dispute: the traditionalists and the nativists. Although they frequently proclaim themselves the antitheses of each other, they follow essentially the same model, varying merely in outward appearances.

The first and oldest actors in Gauchism are the traditionalists. They maintain an organized movement attentive to all that is related to the symbolic goods of the state and try to exercise their control and orientation over these goods. They are joined by intellectuals who write about the movement and who occupy strategic positions. For them it is fundamental to demarcate what the "true" Gaúcho values are; hence their need to make themselves the guardians of tradition. To maintain the distinction between Rio Grande do Sul and Brazil is a way to preserve the state's cultural identity. Therefore, a recurring theme in the traditionalist discourse is the threat hovering over the Gaúcho integrity.

Threats to Gaúcho integrity come from the outside, from the introduction of "alien" customs spread by mass communication, as well as from the inside, through the misrepresentations of "bad" traditionalists, through their inadequate use of artistic groups, through aberrations in the choreographs of Gaúcho dances, and so on. From there springs the imperious need to define what is right and what is wrong, or even better, what is authentic and what is spurious. Therefore, the traditionalists are constantly preoccupied with establishing parameters, separating the pure from the impure, in a process analogous to that described by Mary Douglas in *Purity and Danger*.[18] Thus no amount of care is too great to stop the "trampling in the loss of characterization of culture and customs."[19]

All this preoccupation translates into a search for norms and the elaboration of documents that attempt to design directives. One of the most important examples is the *Manual do Tradicionalismo* (Traditionalist manual) by Glaucus Saraiva, one of the creators and theoreticians of the movement and the author of *Carta de Princípios do Movimento Tradicionalista* (The charter of principles of the traditionalist movement).

It is interesting that the *Manual* begins by affirming that "a large segment of traditionalists do not know what traditionalism is!"

Therefore the manual warns, "demonstrations, parades, exposi-
tions, contests, everything in fact that has a didactic character for
popular consumption and that can be assimilated must loyally follow folkloric criteria, so that we do not distort or leave out characteristics of what exists or existed in our traditions and customs."[20]
However, when one interviews traditionalists, despite their preoccupation with delimiting concepts and parameters, one observes a
great difficulty in defining and distinguishing such terms as *tradition, folklore, regionalism, nativism, Gaúcho culture,* and so on.

True, we are facing a group of intellectuals who yield a certain
amount of knowledge as a form of power. In the final analysis, it is
a matter of who monopolizes the right to affirm what is and what
is not Gaúcho tradition and culture as well as who exercises influence over the marketing of symbolic goods.

One of the questions traditionalists struggled with when they
established their movement was precisely how one establishes
what Gaúcho tradition actually was. Thus scholars began to study
legends, songs, dances, poetry, and clothing. They came to the conclusion, however, that the existing material was scarce:

> When one goes to the Northeast, one finds folklore exemplified
> at every moment in daily life. This does not happen here. If one
> analyzes the Rio Grandian folklore [one verifies that it is] . . . very
> weak in popular manifestations. It is rich in the cult of tradition.
> Proof of this is that one values things the most at the time one
> begins to lose them.[21]

The supposed poverty of Gaúcho folklore does not exactly correspond to reality, but it creates one more way for the intellectuals
to legitimize their need to invent traditions—an activity that may
be easier than researching already existing traditions.[22] Likewise,
one must point out that many traditionalists view as folklore only
that which has been catalogued, thus ignoring popular manifestations that have always existed spontaneously in the state. These
traditionalists have constructed a figure that is frequently outside
reality but one that they "defend" and consider the legitimate representative of Rio Grandian values. The social construction of the
identity of this crystallized Gaúcho comes from the past and is not
subject to great modification.

After participating in the group of Brazilian representatives who
attended the Tradition Day in Montevideo, Uruguay, in 1949, two

of the founders of the '35 CTG, Paixão Côrtes and Barbosa Lessa, came back "disillusioned with our poverty in musical and choreographic themes with a clear traditional stamp. When we arrived here, we conducted a preliminary survey and we verified that—in contrast to the lively northeastern folklore, for example—little or nothing was left to us, in dance." Since no record was left of several of these cultural manifestations, they thought it necessary to invent them. Thus when the '35 CTG was invited to make a presentation at the Third National Week of Folklore in Porto Alegre in 1950, sponsored by the Brazilian branch of UNESCO, the group's imagination gave way:

> Hurriedly we sent for chintz dresses for our sisters and cousins; we tried to reconstruct a *media-canha* [a historic popular dance performed to polka music; today it is one of the versions of the *fandango*] that we had attended in Montevideo, and on the night of the festivities we presented to the public, for the first time, pieces of choreography that we had sniffed here and there: the *Caranguejo* [an old Rio Grandian dance probably of Azorian origin], the *Pezinho* [literally, little foot—another typical Rio Grandian dance that requires intricate footwork on the part of the dancers]. The "Little Foot" was a total novelty. . . . Nevertheless, the public accepted it. What's more, they applauded enthusiastically. Confirming what we would read thirty years later in Eric Hobsbawm: The dance of the "Little Foot" was responding to a need felt not only by our group of young men but also by the spectator public. Having discovered that night the communicative force of popular dance, Paixão Côrtes and I faced a dilemma. Either we would run back to Montevideo to learn instantly with our "eastern brothers" the "Gaúcho dances of the Great Pampas fatherland" or else roll up our sleeves and search Rio Grande do Sul in an attempt to discover melodic and choreographic shards that, conveniently gathered and glued, might approximate our Luso-Brazilian heritage.[23]

Of interest in this quote is the reference to Hobsbawm, an author who criticizes the invention of traditions, as an a posteriori legitimizer of the Gaúcho Traditionalist Movement, thus showing the kind of knowledge the movement's intellectuals have in present-day bibliography.

Upon analyzing the folkloric manifestations in the state, Augusto Meyer criticized the romantic vision that presumed folklore would originate within the popular levels of the population, and he pointed out that "the contribution of the 'people' is relatively *circumspect* in contrast to the creative initiative of the educated minorities."[24]

This becomes clear in the case of the old Gaúcho *fandango* dances, which moved from the rancher's great room to the peons' bunkhouse as the new European dances began to be adopted by the ruling classes. In the words of João Cezimbra Jacques: "Among the ruling classes, the *fandango*, which up until 1839 and 1840 was still popular, began to be replaced by the dances that originated in Europe such as the *ril*, the *gavota*, the *sorongo*, the *montenegro*, the waltz, and later the polka, the *chotes*, the *contradanças*, the mazurkas, and finally the beautiful Spanish *havaneiras*."[25]

This process brings to mind the phenomenon of circularity in the relationship between the culture of the popular classes with that of the ruling classes first described by Bakhtin and again examined in the work of Carlo Ginzburg. These authors show that in preindustrial Europe, there was, between the culture of the upper classes and that of the subaltern classes, a circular relationship formed by reciprocal influences that traveled from top to bottom as well as from bottom to top. In a similar manner, studying the modifications that the Catholic saints went through in Afro-Brazilian religions, Bastide developed the concept of *reinterpretation*, showing how a group may attribute a new meaning to a cultural expression in terms of its own symbolic system.[26]

The traditionalists began inventing and appropriating a series of traditions, some of which became so popular that they were frequently considered as having a folk origin in spite of their originators' claims that they were indeed their own creations. Thus one of the most popular songs composed by Barbosa Lessa and based on the homonymous legend is generally considered part of the state's folklore, to its author's surprise:

"The Little Black Boy Who Tended the Pasture" was a song I wrote when the '35 CTG was just beginning, when we had no music; there was no traditionalist music, no regionalist music, not anything. You could count on one hand [what was available] so we had to compose our own songs, and one of the songs I wrote was "The Little Black Boy Who Tended the Pasture." Later the Farroupilha Group adopted it as a theme song in their television programs and it was heard everywhere and became well known.

Today it practically belongs to the heritage of Rio Grande do Sul and that has given me much satisfaction, since I have made friends through "The Little Black Boy Who Tended the Pasture" and other songs as well. I resent it that Rio Grande do Sul is so backward when it comes to culture. There is no respect for intellectual endeavors, no respect for the artist, and a malicious overtone whenever someone mentions that a writer or a composer has stupidly decided to speak of things from his homeland . . . soon that becomes folklore. The Symphonic Orchestra of Porto Alegre presented "The Little Black Boy Who Tended the Pasture" as having no known composer. One day, they performed on the anniversary of the Anne Frank School at the end of 1978. They rented the Leopoldina Theater for the Anne Frank performance (my daughter studied there), and the announcer said: "And now, by an unknown composer, 'The Little Black Boy Who Tended the Pasture.' " My wife was in the audience and [she thought that] it could have been another "Little Black Boy Who Tended the Pasture," but it was mine. When they finished the performance, she stood up from the audience and said: "Hey . . . the author is not unknown; I sleep with him every night and his name is Barbosa Lessa."[27]

Another area in which much tradition was invented was that of dress, a theme of endless discussions about authenticity. It seems that the *bombacha* [baggy pants]—the key item in the masculine dress—has an interesting trajectory. Glaucus Saraiva, one of the founders of the '35 CTG and author of the *Traditionalist Manual*, argues the following:

[The Gaúcho clothing] is characterized as the most precious typical Brazilian clothing, since, symbolized by the *bombacha*, it is made from cloth of various weights, adaptable to the several different climates in our state. It is the most popular clothing because it is worn in the fields as well as in the city, at fiestas and at formal ceremonies; it is the most democratic garment because it is worn by the peon in the humble farms and by the boss in the mansions in the city; it is the most glorious because, wearing it, the Gaúcho wrote a large part of the history of Rio Grande do Sul and Brazil.[28]

Sérgio da Costa Franco, however, makes this argument:

[The *pilchas* were] work clothes worn generally by the peons and not by the ranchers. The higher layers of rural society always tried to identify with city dwellers, wearing suits with straight pants, ties, short boots, or shoes. There exists, therefore, a component that is not duly underscored in the traditionalist movement: the movement searched for a valorization of the lower levels of rural society; it looked for models of authenticity not in the bosses but in the horsemen, the tamers, the herd peons, the barn hands, and the rodeo hands. The elites did not serve as a model for tradition.[29]

If we can generalize from this, the adoption of clothing would have originated among the popular classes—a debatable issue—even though today the *bombacha* is worn by middle-class urban youth.

Tau Golin has another opinion. He argues that the *bombacha* originated with English mercantilism:

Rare are the registers about the *bombacha* before the Paraguay War. The *bombacha* entered the Prata region thanks to the Crimean War, when English manufacturers produced thousands of uniforms for the Turkish army. However, the conflict ended before it was expected to end, and so many "Turkish pants" were left over. The Prata river market became the salvation for the great losses by selling the pants to the troops in the Triple Alliance. As a demonstration that traditionalism never lives in isolation, the Gaúcho only began wearing the honorable *bombachas* of today because the English mercantilists did not admit a negative balance in their books.[30]

This phenomenon is similar to that shown by Hugh Trevor-Roper when he demonstrated that the *tartan philibeg*, the "traditional" Scottish kilt, appeared only in the eighteenth century:

So, far from being a traditional Highland dress, it was invented by an Englishman after the Union of 1707; the differentiated "clan tartans" are an even later invention. They were designed as part of a pageant devised by Sir Walter Scott in honor of a Hanoverian king, and they owe their present form to two other Englishmen. . . . We may thus conclude that the kilt is a purely modern costume, first designed, first worn, by an English Quaker industrialist, and that it was bestowed by him on the Highlanders in order not to preserve their traditional way of life but to ease its transformation: to bring them out of the heather into the factory.[31]

Leaving aside the discussion about the authenticity of the *bombacha* or about British imposition thereof, it is interesting to verify that after taking care of their own clothing, traditionalists went on to decide what to do with the clothing of women. The traditionalists decided to call the men peons, as a way of designating the activity that the Gaúcho carried out on the ranches. They decided to call the women *prendas*, a word that does not refer to any activity but that means adornment, jewelry, or an object that may be given as a gift. Thus women were reduced to the status of adornments in a process in which man was essentially active and woman was passive. The traditionalists decided that the male garment should reproduce that worn in the fields by the Gaúcho. But the question remained about what to do with the female garment:

> From 1865 until today, there are numerous illustrations of female clothing: in paintings, Daguerrotypes, and photographs. But when the Traditionalist Movement founded the '35 CTG in Porto Alegre on 24 April 1948, the young men (only sometime later did the first young women join) felt the need to create a feminine set of clothing that matched the brilliant masculine garment. Thus they consulted photographs of their own families and were inspired by the simple clothing worn by women who worked in the fields as well as by the Uruguayan traditionalists, and even—although this is hard to believe—the "redneck" dress that they had fought against, and, as a result of all this, they created the now famous "*prenda* dress," within the valid guidelines of the simplest feminine dress in Rio Grande do Sul—the printed calico or chintz—at the end of the nineteenth century and beginning of the twentieth. In spite of it being a traditionalist creation, the *prenda* dress conserved the pattern and seriousness of the model dress of the Gaúcho woman.[32]

Some, however, are of another belief:

> The Gaúcho woman did not and does not have typical clothing. With the development of the Traditionalist Movement and the first young women joining the CTGs, two things were created: the term *prenda* to classify the women symbolically as female associates and, based on old photographs and other research sources, the "*prenda* dress." It was *circumspect* and simple, so that the young women might be able to follow the dress of the "peons" and distinguish themselves as associates of a Center for

Traditions. All of this is nothing more than convention to give the *prendas* a typical dress that they did not know how to maintain throughout our sociological formation, and this was done for a very simple reason: women's universal vanity, always trying to follow the "fashion," no matter where it comes from. And this very feminine impulse has already transformed that *circumspect* and simple "suit" into a thousand and one different dresses with different accessories. We are not going to be the ones who will convince or unravel the universal force of feminine coquettish behavior. We merely plead that our dear traditionalists, attending to the virtue of circumspection, simplicity, and reserve which the Gaúcho has attributed to them, will not transform the "*prenda* dresses" and their accessories into costumes that tempt the moral sense of austerity of our Traditionalist Movement. . . . The function of the feminine dress is to serve as a frame for women's grace and beauty, not to make them look grotesque or ridiculous.[33]

One can perceive in this an attempt not only to place woman in a subaltern position but to control her femininity and sexuality as well. The Traditionalist Movement's emphasis on circumspection and moral austerity reveals a fear of the power women might have, through their behavior, of shaming men and therefore blemishing what the men considered to be their most precious possession: their honor. Therefore, as occurs in other societies, an obsessive preoccupation with the need to control women emerged.

However, in spite of all the regulations about the feminine garment, when women dress in Gaúcho style, they frequently prefer to wear the masculine clothing rather than the *prenda*. For example, Miss Brazil, Ieda Maria Vargas, a woman from Rio Grande do Sul, on becoming Miss Universe in 1963, presented herself abroad wearing a *chiripá*, a Gaúcho garment made up of a strip of material that goes between the legs and is attached to the waist by a leather belt. This was always a male, not a female garment. It is not difficult to understand this preference if we recall that when the traditionalists speak about Rio Grande do Sul, it is always the male figure that is exalted. To the woman remains the subaltern role of *prenda*. When they dress in the male garment, women are appropriating the symbols of prestige that are reserved for the Gaúcho, the representative social figure in a society where women hold a secondary position. This process resembles what occurred with regard to the German and Italian immigrants. As mentioned above, the adoption of the Gaúcho model on the part of these immigrants signified a symbolic form of social upward mobility, since the Gaúcho, with his field expressions and his horse, was perceived as a socially superior type.

During my fieldwork, I had the occasion to witness a scene precisely involving clothing. During the Twenty-seventh Gaúcho Traditionalist Congress, which took place in Campo Bom in January 1982, one of the presenters who spoke from the podium was not wearing traditional clothing. He was interrupted by a participant who admonished him for preaching Gaúcho customs, but coming to an event of that importance without wearing the typical garment. The presenter had an intelligent comeback to the participant's interruption, "Partner, my Gauchism is not in my pants but in my heart!"

Frequently the revival of Gaúcho culture is seen as a victory for traditionalism. Of course this "victory" trips on the fact that the new artists are reelaborating Rio Grandian themes without adhering to any kind of dogma and at times are even parodying the traditional figure of the Gaúcho. This reelaboration occurs through the humorists, such as Luís Fernando Veríssimo, creator of the *Analyst from Bagé*,[34] a book that had spectacular sales (78 editions were published and more than 250,000 copies sold from its initial publication in October 1981 until October 1983; from the perspective of Brazilian publication standards, it was an impressive best-seller). In the book Veríssimo provides a symbiosis between the roughness and the macho image of the inhabitant of Bagé (a city in the *Campanha* region) and the sophistication associated with psychoanalysis. The macho image was also satirized by Rio Grandian composers Kleiton and Kledir. After having produced songs such as "Maria Fumaça" [Steam engine], which was introduced at the Festival '79 on the Tupi Television Network and became a mark of the "nationalization" of Gaúcho music, they wrote "Trova" [Ballad], a satire that speaks of the "Gaúcho bunda mole" [literally "soft buttocks," an insult meaning an idiot, someone with little intelligence; in Rio Grande do Sul, calling a man "bunda mole" means that one does not consider him very virile] causing a city councilman from Porto Alegre to lodge a formal complaint against the song in the Municipal Chamber. But the action backfired since he was called the "city councillor cuca mole" [*cuca* is a slang word for head or mental ability]. The reelaboration created by the new artists becomes apparent even in their garments, when, for example, Kleiton and Kledir appear wearing *bombacha* and tennis shoes—an action considered heresy from an orthodox point of view since the traditional Gaúcho wears boots or canvas shoes, but a manner of dress that corresponds to the customs of the youth.

The Gaúcho Traditionalist Movement cannot control all cultural expressions in the state nor can it hegemonically disseminate its messages. These are different times, engendering different notions of what it means to be a Gaúcho, notions that do not necessarily correspond to the beliefs of the CTGs. The market for symbolic goods has increased, and new actors have begun to claim positions in it.

The music festivals are arenas where much of the debate about what it means to be Gaúcho takes place. The California of Rio Grandian Native Song is an example of this. It takes place annually in December in Uruguaiana, a city in the *Campanha* that is on the Argentina border. Sponsored by the Sinuelo do Pago Center for Gaúcho Traditions, the California was the first of the Gaúcho music festivals and it has served as a model for dozens of festivals that take place in the state.

The growth of the California from the time of its creation in 1971 is impressive. Today it brings together hundreds of composers who compete for prizes and for the possibility of having their compositions included in a recording of all the finalists' compositions. Thousands of people go to Uruguaiana to attend the festival and most of them camp in a "Tent City," a large campground where the campers take part in barbecues, drink *mate* tea, tell "tall tales," and listen to the music of the festival.

As participation in the event increased, its organizers found themselves impelled to define what Gaúcho music is. Thus the rules for the Eleventh California, taking place in December 1981, stated, "We understand the meaning of music from Rio Grande do Sul to be that which evinces the theme of the Gaúcho homeland, based on its folkloric rhythms."[35] The rules state that the competing compositions are evaluated by the Judging Committee "in three different verses, all obligatory and necessarily based on folk rhythms from Rio Grande do Sul. These areas are defined as (a) *country verse*—that which identifies itself with the man, the environment, and the customs of the countryside in Rio Grande do Sul; (b) *Rio Grandian manifestation verse*—that which focuses on other sociocultural and geographic aspects of Rio Grande do Sul not strictly limited to the countryside; and (c) *verse of folkloric representation*—that which stems from the verses defined in items (a) and (b) above and projects itself universally as an art in terms of its poetic and musical treatment."[36]

Among the objectives of the California is that of "discovering new paths for the true music of Rio Grande do Sul, through the present-day language of Gaúcho origins and constants."[37] The problem, naturally, is how does one define what the state's "true" music is. This question has generated heated polemics that culminated in the episode of the *Uruguaiana Charter* on the occasion of the Eleventh California. The Triage Committee of that California, meeting before the festival, introduced a document entitled *Uruguaiana Charter*, "with no other motive than that of attempting to collaborate on the improvement of Rio Grandian music of native extraction."[38]

Among other salient points in the *Charter* with regard to the compositions of the most recent Californias, we find "repetition of themes linked to Gaúcho tradition and folklore; exhaustive and generally inadequate usage of certain Gaúcho themes; compulsion with the past and with infancy as a background for the lyrics; scarce focus on the contemporary human and socioeconomic realities in Rio Grande do Sul; repetitive use of clichés; rare utilization of certain rhythms, and utilization of foreign rhythms."[39]

One of the disqualified composers (of the 297 compositions entered in the contest, 36 were chosen) decided to present *The Uruguaiana Anti-Charter*, in which he contests the arguments of the *Uruguaiana Charter*. After refuting the *Charter*'s arguments one by one, the author concludes: "As one reads in objective 'C' of the regulation of the California of the Rio Grandian Native Song, they are trying to 'discover new paths for the true music in RS.' What is the path? Does anyone know it? It seems there must be someone who knows it . . . or is there not?"[40]

The regulations of the California also point out that "the Organizing Committee of the Eleventh California of Rio Grandian Native Song, with the intention of preserving the seriousness with which one searches for and revitalizes the values and characters of Gaúcho culture, will not permit the participation of persons or groups wearing an incomplete Gaúcho garment or those with features that render it uncharacteristic."[41] Every year certain musicians are invited to participate in evening presentations although they are not competing for the awards. During the Eleventh California, one of the invited groups was *Os Tapes* who had won the Second California but subsequently had developed a rather critical vision of the festival and a musical project quite distant from the vision of the Gaúcho Traditionalist Movement. Since they were not competing, and therefore not subject to the regulations, the group decided deliberately not to wear Gaúcho garments. When I had the occasion of interviewing them, they assured me that they saw no reason to present themselves "in costume" as Gaúchos from the frontier, since they were from Tapes, a small city a hundred kilometers from Porto Alegre at Lagoa dos Patos, a region where there is rice cultivation.

It is significant that such polemics almost always surround music festivals. It is in this arena that the actors of Gauchism come to battle, with music as the instrument of dispute. Music festivals have become privileged arenas where one can study the conflicts that surround the construction of Gaúcho identity inasmuch as they are the outlet for antagonistic positions struggling against one another. It is there we witness controversies about musical styles, regional accents,[42] garments, and so on. In the final analysis, all these polemics deal with what Gaúcho culture is and who has the competence to define it. During my fieldwork, there were even occasions when I was asked to intervene to give the "word of the university" in the several disputes being waged by different groups.[43]

The other group of contenders in this polemic is formed basically by artists and journalists who call themselves *nativists* and who do not accept the control and the patronage imposed by the Gaúcho Traditionalist Movement. A constant dispute rages between these two groups, which can be illustrated with a quasi-manifesto article entitled "Ayatollahs of Tradition," written by two journalists who cover musical movements in the state. For these journalists:

> The ayatollahs of tradition . . . are already risking resurrecting dogmas and reliving authoritarian forms of thinking, and little by little they come to judge themselves as proprietors of the manifestations that have something to do with Gaúcho singing. They

occupy posts of influence in the festival organizations and in their judging committees, are active within the systems of communication, and in official institutions of all kinds. And most of the time they are always closing, limiting, and dictating rules and forms of behavior, at times aggressively attacking those who did not learn how to read with their primer.

And they go on:

It cannot be said that a Nativist Movement exists by right, but it is undeniable that it exists in fact. The nativist is not dogmatic, he is not linked to preestablished criteria, and he knows that besides Rio Grande do Sul, other Brazilian states exist, and that beyond Brazil, another world. In music, he wants to experiment, invent, create, without someone permanently telling him that such and such a thing is all right and another is not. The nativist believes that guitars and synthesizers are merely musical instruments, neither diabolical nor corrupting. He also wants the freedom to be influenced by other musical ideas in peace, as occurred with his ancestors in the nineteenth century. These ancestors enlivened the musical field with rhythms that came from European centers and these rhythms were transformed by other personalities who were regional and unique. The nativists want to dress however they wish, not according to canons and traditionalist figurines. The nativists have before them today's reality and they know that the very exalted (and ironically also ostracized) peons, of whom the ayatollahs of tradition speak, are not happily roaming the fields. These peons work very hard wearing *bombachas* or mended pants, not wearing shiny boots but mundane thongs. Or else they walk the roads or stay in camps for the landless. The nativists are in favor of agrarian reform, of a more just social order, and are against the latifundia and the almost slavelike system that still persists. The nativists do not agree with the hierarchy that is fed and defended by the traditionalists, as if the world were a large barracks. The nativists know they have a past, but they do not worship this past as a way to distance themselves from the present, nor do they worship mystifying heroes who are already fossilized, as if Rio Grande do Sul were parked in the beginning of the century. . . . Certain traditions need to be preserved, and in this the CTGs fulfill their role. But to encamp the Rio Grandian festivals as the property of the Traditionalist Movement is an aberration. To encircle Gaúcho music and artistic manifestations within a barbed-wire fence is something we cannot understand or permit. The agropastoral world has weakened with the inevitable industrial growth. Urban centers have swelled with the uncontrollable avalanche of the rural exodus. Meanwhile, the ayatollahs of tradition, all well placed in the cities, want to revive and maintain the music of the countryside, under the fleeting argument that it was there that the peons had a home, food, and happiness—a mystical ideal fed by farmers who lost a stable and disciplined labor force. But why did these people leave the country to become, today, unqualified workers in civil construction, paper workers, washer women, domestic maids, and prostitutes, bringing forth abandoned children and assailants, illiterates without roots, guerrilla fighters of the lowest class. Those who fled the countryside imagined they would find better days. And of course they did not find them. The ayatollahs want to sing of their ideal past, not of their drama. Evidently it will not be with sweet words nor with metaphors that one will achieve that. However, it needs to be done, in a rhythm that most closely approaches the reality of the mud in the marginal villages. At no time does this stop them from singing of their passion, sex, love, and whatever may stimulate daily life.[44]

The document had great repercussions and several people supported it.[45] As a comeback, one of those who wore the cap of the "ayatollah of tradition" called them cowbirds in an interview:

I believe they are tradition's cowbirds. A cowbird does not make a nest but lays eggs in other birds' nests and waits until they hatch. They have no ideological or affective commitment to Gauchism. When they saw that nativism was a phenomenon that was opening and enlarging its space, they entered and took their piece of cake. My dream is to hear the criticism of those who are identified ideologically with Gauchism; people who know the cause, not outsiders or foreigners who are riding the wave of success and who will promptly abandon nativism if nativism were to enter a wave of decline.[46]

Besides the tone of resentment, one can perceive a pretension of ownership of tradition justified by having helped create it and transform it into a cult.

An accomplished nativist composer and poet also entered into the debate when he published an article criticizing what he called "cultural patronage" and "folkloric patrol":

Regional culture took its conservative option. In order for this to have happened, it took all the ideological support of the CTGs. Add to this the phenomenon that at great risk I called "cultural patronage." I referred to the fact that the organizers and promoters of the festivals were gradually assuming a posture of ideologues and censors of artistic creation. The selection committees for the compositions had become "commissions of inquiry." . . . In the general plan, a "folkloric patrol" takes hold of dogmatic and absolute truths to determine what is native, Gaúcho, and valid in terms of regional music. They are people dedicated to traditionalism. However, I can affirm that they do not know who Pablo Picasso is, they hate Piazzola, and they think that Fellini is a brand of macaroni.[47]

Besides criticizing the traditionalists' role as censors of Gaúcho art, the nativist composer throws darts at them for their roughness and ignorance with respect to everything that is outside the narrow circle of their cultural world.[48]

Other nativist composers participated in this polemic. Thus a nativist composer who had been an award winner in several festivals proclaimed the following:

For the traditionalists, the music of Rio Grande do Sul must be marked with "scenes of implicit coarseness," since they will never admit in their explicit discourse that the authentic Gaúcho they proclaim must be rude—with the ability to withstand the roughness of the field work—and servile, to subordinate himself to the masters "of soul and the Pampas." . . . The new musicians rebel precisely against the conservative reductionism that does not recognize Gaúcho legitimacy for another type of music that is made by today's Gaúchos, who are not the centaurs of the Pampas but the keyboarders of the future in the dawn of the information era, or they are disinherited from the land in the pursuit of justice. Those who take a nativist stance vindicate a democratic life-style that includes different manifestations of today's Rio Grandian music, without discriminations, catalogues, stamps, and prescriptions.[49]

During the music festivals a constant dispute is brewing between the traditionalists and the nativists. The latter believe that their style is just the opposite of the former, which is labeled "nheco-nheco culture" [this is the onomatopoetic depiction of a musical rhythm that is very poor; therefore, when referring to culture, this means a musical culture that does not introduce innovations, such as the electric guitar], meaning one that is poor in resources, grounded only in the accordion, without making use of any electronic resources, and tied to well-beaten themes from the past. The traditionalists, on the other hand, invoke their authority from their having been the creators of the first festivals and the processors of the revival of all things Gaúcho. These differences, besides generating heated debates, do not run deep, however, since the traditionalists and the nativists both deal with the same theme. In the words of Rosângela Araújo, who conducted in-depth research about the music festivals:

> The "nativists'" songs present themselves as more innovative than those of the "traditionalists" in the aspect of their contemporary themes and style of rhythm. However, in essence they follow the same "pattern," the design changing only in the details. Thus both factions have as a base images of the "countryside" as a habitat par excellence of the typical regional human figure. For a child of traditionalism, nativism does not seem to be its antithesis, as some would like it to be, nor is it traditionalism itself as others would like it to be, but merely an offshoot dressed in new clothing, under the influence of some ideas from its time.[50]

In this sense it is interesting that the nativists interpret the surge of Gaúcho music in a way similar to the traditionalists, and they characterize it as a defense against external dangers. Thus Luís Coronel believes:

> It is a reaction of regional culture against the process of cultural massification that occurred in Brazil, primarily through the superdevelopment of electronic production, electronic media, and cultural centralization via television. It seems that the Gaúcho reacted to all this by attempting to return to his roots. Regionalism is a defense strategy in Brazilian culture, via regional culture. If Gaúcho youth, as well as all Gaúchos, did not turn to their local culture, they would be swallowed up by the great national media . . . television shows from Globo [Network] and everything else.[51]

Another well-known nativist composer agrees with this line of interpretation:

> Rio Grande do Sul did not escape the internationalization of the economy and culture (through the famous multinational corporations and the institution of a globalizing cultural industry) that generated the economic and cultural de-nationalization with the negation and confinement of the so-called regional subcultures. This had immediate and significant effects in our state. We began to suffer a double colonization: one external, with the imposition of North American cultural patterns, and the other internal, through the so-called "global patterns of culture." For these reasons, the movement of "regeneration" in Rio Grande do Sul, which is showing itself today, is one of the offshoots through which we hope to reconquer our cultural identity. And this is manifested in nativist music, literature, historiography, in plastic arts, cinema, dance, as well as in journalism, the theater, and so on. Thus the Gaúcho middle class is once again Gaúcho, taking hold of a new regionalism, constituted of certain elements that reaffirm past values and others that both negate them and surpass them.[52]

That this debate is taking place among urban, middle-class intellectuals is clear in the research conducted by Rosângela Araújo. When she analyzed from a sample the social origins of the composers in the most important state music festivals, she found that only 20 percent of them lived the daily country life of their youth or adolescence. The majority were born and reared in cities. These cities were predominantly in the interior, and frequently in the *Campanha* region—a fact used to justify knowledge of country life. As for family origins, most of the composers come from groups with some economic and cultural capital, thus reflecting the fact that 85 percent of them had attended a university and only 15 percent make a living from their music alone.[53]

If one weighs the polemics, the differences between traditionalists and nativists are a matter of style. The former almost deliberately assume a more conservative and less developed position, whereas the latter appear more progressive and innovative, intending to bridge the state's past and present. What they have in common, besides the preoccupation with Gaúcho roots, is that they fight for the same market of symbolic goods and access to recognition, such as the music festivals, journalistic debates, and so on. In a certain way they could be characterized as intellectuals who are on the periphery of the established circles of intellectual legitimization, insofar as they do not have access to the classic institutions, such as universities, academic journals, scientific congresses, and so forth.

One could well imagine that with all the strength traditionalism possesses, the movement could involve itself directly in politics by electing its members to political offices. In fact, the Gaúcho Traditionalist Movement is courted by candidates from all political spheres at the time of elections. The traditionalist leaders I interviewed, however, are emphatic in reminding us that the *Charter of Principles* affirms the movement's independence from political parties, and they point out that, until now, those members who tried to get elected using the movement's militancy were not successful. During the 1986 election, for example, several candidates were running for parliamentary office from different parties, among them a former president of the Gaúcho Traditionalist Movement. One of the candidates for federal representative was a well-known traditionalist leader, from the Partido do Movimento Democrático Brasileiro (PMDB), a party that, during the wake of the Cruzado Plan,[54] succeeded in having a great number of representatives elected. In addition, he was the announcer of a weekly Sunday program of Gaúcho music for the largest television network in Rio Grande do Sul; he had a weekly column about regionalism in the largest state newspaper, and he participated in radio programs. He affirmed that, once elected, he would always arrive at the House of Representatives wearing the traditional Gaúcho garment, and if he were stopped from carrying out his parliamentary duties wearing the typical dress, he would enter a motion to modify the House rules. With all these appeals, increased by his access to the means of communication, one would assume he would easily be elected. In reality, though, none of the candidates "wearing *bombacha* and boots" were successful in the election. Analyzing the election results in his column, he stated that, on the one hand, this could be viewed as lamentable since the members of the Gaúcho Traditionalist Movement form a great legion that is always networking with politicians, but on the other hand, it could be explained in this way:

The Gaúcho movement has traditionally been averse to party politics and has prohibited such discussions within the confines of
traditionalist bunkhouses, a fact, after all, that is expressed in the
Charter of Principles. The traditionalists feel somewhat used,
somewhat exploited, when a candidate tries to win their votes "in
their role as traditionalists," even if the candidate is one of their
companions in the cause. Any political propaganda inside the
bunkhouses is harshly rejected. . . . From this one can explain the
maxim, "traditionalists do not vote for traditionalists."[55]

Obviously some intellectuals are preoccupied with analyzing the
traditionalist and nativist ideologies. With regard to the former,
what is often pointed out is the backward character of their world-
view (contained in the principal thesis of the movement, *The
Meaning and Value of Traditionalism*), the conservative nature of
the organization, and the symbology that the CTGs use to reproduce the structure of the ranches (adopting names for leadership
positions such as boss, foreman, etc., while the members are called
peons), and primarily their proximity to the current governing
power. Thus the fact that the *Charter of Principles*, written by
Glaucus Saraiva and approved in the Seventh Traditionalist Congress that took place in Taquara in 1961, emphasizes social har-
mony, the collective good, cooperation with the state, respect for
laws, and a civic spirit[56] causes the movement to be frequently
characterized as ideological and attempting to maintain in a state
of submission those members of the rural masses and the popular
layers of society who migrated to the cities. In the words of Golin,
one of the movement's sharpest critics, "The Gaúcho Traditionalist Movement, being perfected for more than a century, articulates
itself through an ideology that is necessarily unifying. Exploiters
and exploited defend the same principles in their comprehension
of the world." He argues that "the deep barrier in which traditionalism constituted itself is more than evident, and it creates obstacles in the fight of the proletariat. This being the case, it serves as
a strong component against the new society."[57] Even though his
analysis is directed more toward traditionalists, Golin also criticizes the nativists. He coined a term to unite the two categories:
"I consider as *tradinativists* those who fight for traditionalism
and/or nativism, as worshipers and/or creators, without having
any real personal anxiety that they are heading for a rupture with

the traditional culture that is ontologically hegemonic in Rio
Grande do Sul."[58]

From a similar perspective, Dacanal, speaking of the "afterlife of
the ideological constructions of Gaúcho oligarchy," affirms that
Gaúcho mythology "still ruled sovereign in the 1970s when Rio
Grande do Sul was already integrated not only in Brazilian modern
urban-industrial society, but also in the international capitalist
macrosystem." However, he states:

> As for the future of the CTGs, it appears to me that they are dete-
> riorating. Having lost their initial social function, they are tend-
> ing toward—and indeed already are—losing the function they
> had in the 1970s and 1980s, marching toward a progressive dis-
> appearance, subsumed by the general jellylike mixture of plane-
> tary-multinational-industrial-urban culture. This does not mean
> that the historic themes of Rio Grande do Sul cannot once again
> be the subject of a poetic and musical renovation, as in fact the
> nativists have shown very well.[59]

For this author, "traditionalists and nativists are, if not flour
from the same bag, at least two sides of the same coin." And
therefore:

> There seems to be no reason for any problems to exist between
> traditionalists and nativists. On the contrary, one could say they
> should feel like allies in their fight to preserve their own cultural
> identity. Why, then, did the polemic explode? The answer is this:
> In spite of being products of the same historic-cultural situation,
> traditionalists and nativists undertook—and some continue to
> undertake—a true dialogue among deaf people, and paradoxically
> on the same theme, the Rio Grandian past, a past to which the
> traditionalists stick desperately in an attempt to immobilize the
> wheel of history. It is a past over which the nativists shed their
> tears, accepting emotionally the inevitability of the passage of
> time, by perceiving it as doubly discrepant.[60]

It is interesting that traditionalism and nativism, through the
perspective of this type of criticism, are seen as very efficacious ideologies but at the same time anachronistic, since there would be a
discrepancy between their creations based on the state's past and
present-day reality. This creates a curious situation at the very
least if we remember that the efficacy of a discourse is related to its

verisimilitude and to its capacity of repercussion in the imaginary of the social actors. How, then, can a discourse be simultaneously anachronistic and efficacious? Where is the contradiction? In the sender or the receiver of the message? Or is it in the interpretation of those who analyze the process?

At first sight it may seem strange to find this revival of Gauchism at the turn of the century when Brazil is well integrated politically, economically, culturally, and in its transportation and mass communication networks. A growing economic, political, and administrative centralization, as well as the development of sophisticated communication networks, are frequently considered responsible for the weakening of regional power and the deepening of homogeneity and standardizing of habits and attitudes in the population. In spite of—or perhaps because of—this growing centralization, one observes today in Brazil tendencies that are contrary to this process, tendencies that manifest themselves through the affirmation of regional identities with Rio Grande do Sul as an expressive example.

Significantly, Gauchism gains strength again when Rio Grande do Sul, a state with a firm rural past but whose population is mainly urban, feels it is increasingly losing its importance in Brazil, a country that has accentuated its centralizing tendencies at the political and economic levels as well as at the cultural level.

If Gauchism rewrites rural tradition and life, it does so in an urbanized state that wishes to be modern. It may seem curious that this movement should take hold of rural and past values when Rio Grande do Sul is predominantly urban and quite industrialized. This fact has made some consider the phenomenon as a mere passing fashion or as an anachronistic ideology, albeit curiously efficacious, something like the concept of survivals previously mentioned.[61] However, because of the extension and duration of the phenomenon, it is difficult to label it as a fashion or as an ideology that has passed its time. With regard to the aspect of fashion that publicity can attribute to any phenomenon, this is far more lasting than other waves. At the same time, although a considerable number of intellectuals point to the ideological and reactionary aspect of the return to an idyllic time that either never existed or no longer exists, this denouncement does not resolve the question either. In this sense, for example, it is difficult to explain why a state in which a conservative ideology would be hegemonic has an oppositionist political tradition.

It happens that the movement is far from losing energy, which corresponds to a tendency that has lately been occurring in Brazil. With the political opening that began at the end of the 1970s, one observed an intense process of establishing new political actors and building new social identities. Inasmuch as identities are representations formulated in opposition or in contrast to other identities, what is sought is precisely the differences. Thus the construction of these identities goes through the elaboration of traits in Brazilian culture that are appropriated and used as diacritical marks, that is, as signals that confer a mark of distinction on different social groups.

One could draw a parallel between what is presently occurring in Rio Grande do Sul and what occurred with the modernist movement that began in São Paulo. The intellectuals of the Week of Modern Art in 1922, at an early time in the movement, emphasized the question of an artistic and cultural modernization in Brazil but, beginning with the second phase of the movement (1924 on), the modernists realized they would only achieve the universal through the national and an attack against backwardness was substituted for an emphasis on the elaboration of a national culture, thereby bringing about a rediscovery of Brazil by Brazilians.[62]

What is happening in Rio Grande do Sul seems to indicate that today, for the Gaúcho, the national is achieved through the regional, that is, the people of Rio Grande do Sul can only be Brazilian if they are Gaúcho first. Gaúcho identity is nowadays no longer formulated in terms of the *Farroupilha* tradition, but through the expression of a cultural distinction in a country where the means of mass communication tend to homogenize society culturally through standards that often originate on the beaches of southern Rio de Janeiro.

When one attempts to compare Rio Grande do Sul to the rest of the country, pointing to differences and constructing a social identity, it is almost inevitable that this process will reach out to the state's rural past and to the figure of the Gaúcho, since these are the distinguishing emblems of the state.

Chapter Six

NEW FRONTIERS IN CULTURE

●

At the turn of this century the world is witnessing two processes that are occurring simultaneously. On the one hand, there has been a gradual development of a *supra-state*, the European Union. It is the product of the gradual association of several countries that historically were at war with one another and now are associating freely. This union also implies the abolition of economic and labor market borders, the creation of a single monetary unit, the integration of armies, and more important, a pact of renouncing war as a form of resolving conflict among its members. The association of these countries does not mean, however, that ethnic and regional conflicts have disappeared. In several member countries, some of which are apparently quite consolidated, the national question has not been resolved, as can be seen in the separatist movements of the Basques, the Irish, and other nationalities who do not consider themselves represented in the countries to which they belong.

On the other hand, in Eastern Europe and the former Soviet Union, there has been a collapse of countries and the resurgence of ethnic and regional conflicts through an exacerbated nationalism, both causing fratricidal wars. Some of these countries began to disintegrate from the moment there was no longer a repressive regime maintaining different nationalities together under the same nation-state.

Nowadays Brazil it is not affected by regional or ethnic conflicts, but it is beginning to experience some debate along these lines. Brazilians do not want to be part of the Third World, but they also do not belong to the First. Sometimes they experience the presence of groups that want to separate the more advanced regions of the country from those that are less developed. Attempts are made to separate the "South" from the Northeast, and the state of Rio Grande do Sul (including, at times, the states of Santa Catarina and Paraná) from the rest of Brazil. When the economic situation becomes more difficult, this type of proposal gains strength and is presented as a solution to the problems, without taking into account, for example, that the Northeast has furnished the cheap labor needed by the industry in São Paulo and that the Brazilian economy is nationally integrated. It is difficult to imagine its fragmentation.

These contradictory situations are the result of a series of processes that the world has experienced. In the last two hundred years, we have witnessed the formation of nation-states based on the idea of a union of people with similar feelings and interests who live in a delimited territory and whose geographic and symbolic borders must be carefully preserved. The nation-state tends to be against the maintenance of regional and cultural differences, and it demands strict loyalty to the idea of one country.

It so happens that the concept of nation-state is being affected by the compression of time and space, inasmuch as the speed of information and of displacements has intensified and made changes come faster and faster.

Although from the time of the great maritime voyages of the Modern Age it only made sense to envision the economy as a world system, since there already was an exchange of commodities from one continent to another, today we are witnessing a transnationalization of the economy. There was a time when the various national markets consolidated and the key countries tried to export thei͏ erchandise to other countries. Today the economy, even an being multinationalized, is characterized by large cor- with capital being spread out in different nations. These ns frequently sell more commodities outside than inside their country of origin, and they recruit executives from any part of the world according to criteria related to efficiency and not to nationality. For this type of economy, it does not make sense to use the term *national* as a production or consumption category.

Similarly, the dissemination of new communication technologies, like the satellite, the computer, the FAX, and electronic mail, allows for faster and more agile decision making that can be undertaken without hindrance from geographic distances.

It is natural that all these processes are also reflected in the realm of culture. The speed of the dissemination of messages is creating globalized life-styles. Some patterns of consumption and taste are becoming international, for example, rock music, the great festivals, the fashions of the youth, fast foods, and shopping centers. We are also seeing the development of hybrid cultures.[1] In the past, cultures tended to be associated with a particular territory and with specifically defined identities. What we see today is a crossing of cultural and symbolic borders that causes a de-territorialization of cultural phenomena. A symbolic manifestation arises within a certain context—such as rock music—then migrates to other contexts and is ultimately incorporated into another context. Of course these developments are not passive and always imply a reelaboration.

This process of cultural globalization not only gives us the impression of living in a global village but once again poses the question of tradition, of nation, and of region. As the world becomes more complex and more internationalized, the question of differences again arises and an intense process of identity formation occurs. Just as the national unification that occurred in the past confronted the maintenance of regional and cultural diversity, today's world is, in part, witnessing precisely the affirmation of differences. This is happening as much in those countries where the nation-state resulted in a forced integration of different nationalities that do not see themselves represented by their nation and try to constitute themselves into autonomous countries (a process that is occurring in Eastern Europe and in the former Soviet Union), as well as in nations that have united slowly and by their own determination.

Thus, just as the peasants who lived in France in the eighteenth century had difficulty imagining themselves as French citizens, a status given to them through the 1789 Revolution, we can surmise that the inhabitants of the European Union will have difficulty identifying themselves as Europeans, such a large category, and, for the time being, not as significant as identifying oneself as a French citizen, an Italian citizen, and so on. As the world shrinks, it becomes more and more difficult to identify oneself in such generic categories as Europe, the world, and so on. It is natural therefore that social actors look for closer objects with which to identify. We are all citizens of the world, inasmuch as we belong to the human race, but we need points of reference that are near to us. We experience the same difficulty a child has in understanding the meaning of a world map when the child's house is not drawn on it.

It is understandable that in times of crisis and social transformation, there is a rebirth and frequently an invention of traditions. That these traditions have nothing to do with the present situation is irrelevant, for the criteria for analyzing them cannot be their anachronism but what they represent in the imaginary of the groups that cultivate the traditions.

Brazil, in a way, is going through a similar process. One can argue that the country has a certain difficulty in accepting cultural diversity. Brazil is generally administered from "Oiapoque to Chuí" [roughly translated: "From sea to shining sea"] without regard to the regional differences between these two boundaries. Brazilians consider themselves to be citizens of the largest Catholic country in the world, in which one language is spoken, and in which the samba and Carnival in Rio de Janeiro are expressions of national identity. That there has been increasing urbanization and integration through mass media points to the emphasis on cultural homogeneity that heightens even more the idea of uniformity of habits and attitudes in the population. What one misses in this type of representation is cultural diversity. In reality, what is happening in Brazil along with this growing integration is the affirmation of different types of identities. Among them one finds regional identities that make salient the regions' differences in relation to the rest of Brazil as a form of cultural distinction in a country where the mass media tend to homogenize society culturally.

It is precisely at the time Brazil finds itself quite integrated politically, economically, and technologically that it becomes imperative to rethink the question of cultural diversity.

NOTES

1. Nation and Tradition at the Turn of the Millennium

1. Marcel Mauss, "La Nation," in *Oeuvres*, book 3 (Paris: Editions des Minuit, 1969), pp. 593–94.

2. Emile Durkheim, *The Elementary Forms of the Religious Life* (New York: Free Press, 1965), p. 236.

3. Ibid., p. 236.

4. In 1989 the Supreme Court of the United States decided by a vote of 5 to 4 that one has the legal right to burn the North American flag as an act of political protest. The court interpreted the act as an exercise of the right of free speech assured by the Constitution. This highly polemic decision resulted in some groups wishing to propose an amendment to the Constitution explicitly prohibiting the burning of the flag. See VEJA, *Chama da Liberdade* [Flame of freedom] 22, no. 25 (28 June 1989): 62–63.
In German, the term for desertion is *Fahnen Flucht*, that is, flight from the flag, in a metonymic process that equates the flag to one's fatherland.

5. Claude Lévi-Strauss, *The Savage Mind* (London: Weidenfeld and Nicolson, 1966), p. 107.

6. Roger C. Poole, introduction to *Totemism*, by Claude Lévi-Strauss (Harmondsworth: Penguin, 1969), p. 62.

7. Mariza G. S. Peirano, "Etnocentrismo às Avessas: O Conceito de 'Sociedade Complexa'" [Ethnocentrism in reverse: The concept of "complex society"], *Dados* 26, no. 1 (1983): 110.

8. Eric J. Hobsbawm, *Nations and Nationalism Since 1780: Programme, Myth, Reality* (Cambridge: Cambridge University Press, 1992).

9. Benedict Anderson, *Imagined Communities: Reflections on the Origin and Spread of Nationalism* (New York: Verso, 1991), p. 6.

10. Max Weber, "The Nation," in H. H. Gerth and C. Wright Mills, eds., *From Max Weber: Essays in Sociology* (New York: Oxford University Press, 1976), p. 176.

11. Ernest Gellner, *Nations and Nationalism* (Ithaca: Cornell University Press, 1983), p. 56.

12. Robert Darnton, *The Great Cat Massacre and Other Episodes in French Cultural History* (New York: Vintage, 1985), p. 23.

13. Antonio Gramsci, "The Southern Question," in *The Modern Prince and Other Writings* (New York: International Publishers, 1975), p. 31.

14. José Carlos Mariátegui, "Regionalism and Centralism," in *Seven Interpretive Essays on Peruvian Reality* (Austin: University of Texas Press, 1971), p. 153.

15. Michel Rocard, "La région: Une idée neuve pour la gauche," *Pouvoirs* 19 (1981): 132.

16. Ann R. Markusen, "Região e Regionalismo: Um enfoque marxista" [Region and regionalism: A Marxist approach], in *Espaço e Debates* [Space and debates] 1, no. 2 (1981): 83.

17. Ibid., pp. 74–75.

18. Pierre Bourdieu, "L'identité et la représentation: Eléments pour une réflexion critique sur l'idée de région" [Identity and representation: Elements toward a critical reflection on the idea of region], *Actes de la Recherche en Sciences Sociales* 35 (1980): 69.

19. Maurice Halbwachs, *Les cadres sociaux de la mémoire* (Social framework of memory). (Paris: Presses Universitaires de France, 1968).

20. Michael Pollack, "Memória, esquecimento, silêncio" [Memory, forgetting, silence], *Estudos Históricos*, no. 3 (1989): 3.

21. Renato Ortiz. *Cultura Brasileira e Identidade Nacional* [Brazilian culture and national identity] (São Paulo: Brasiliense, 1985), p. 137.

22. Tylor used the term *survivals* to designate "processes, customs, opinions, and so forth, which have been carried on by force of habit into a new state of society different from that in which they had their original home, and they thus remain as proofs and examples of an older condition of culture out of which a newer one has been evolved" (Edward Burnett Tylor, *Primitive Culture* (London: Murray, 1913), vol. 1, p. 16; originally published in 1871).

23. Eunice Ribeiro Durham, "A Dinâmica Cultural na Sociedade Moderna" [Cultural dynamics in modern society], *Ensaios de Opinião*, 2–2 (1977): 33.

24. José Guilherme Cantor Magnani, "Ideologia, lazer e cultura popular: Um estudo do circo-teatro nos bairros de periferia de São Paulo" [Ideology, leisure, and popular culture: A study of the theatre-circus in the neighborhoods in the periphery of São Paulo], *Dados* 23, no. 2 (1980): 183.

25. Eric Hobsbawm, introduction to *The Invention of Tradition* by Eric Hobsbawm and Terence Ranger (Cambridge: Cambridge University Press, 1993), pp. 2–3.

26. Ibid., p. 12.

27. Eric Hobsbawm, "Mass-Producing Traditions: Europe, 1870–1914," in Hobsbawm and Ranger, *The Invention of Tradition*, p. 316.

28. Alan Dundes, "Nationalistic Inferiority Complexes and the Fabrication of Fakelore: A Reconsideration of Ossian, the *Kinder-und Hausmärchen*, the *Kalevala*, and Paul Bunyan," *Journal of Folklore Research* 22, no. 1 (1985): 12.

29. Richard M Dorson, "Fakelore," *Zeitschrift für Volkskunde* 65 (1969): 60; Dundes, "Nationalistic Inferiority Complexes," p. 5.

30. Dundes, "Nationalistic Inferiority Complexes, pp. 10, 13. In 1990 the British Museum presented an exhibit, *False! The Art of Deceiving*, that "not only shows falsification in art, but points out in a general way that counterfeiting is an inseparable dimension of culture from its beginning until today, involving religion, politics, history, journalism, and science. . . . The spirit of the exhibit, far from trying to ridicule the false works or those 'connoisseurs' who were fooled by them, is to try to reflect on the ambiguous status of counterfeits. One only falsifies that which is desired; therefore, even if the false object is an imposture in relation to an original or to the past, it is, on the other hand, highly revealing of the tastes and fantasies that are predominant at the moment in which it is produced. In this sense, it is a fundamental index for the history of tastes in each period. The imposture carries its own truth" (Nicolau Sevcenko, "Mostra revê o valor das falsificações" [Exhibit revisits the value of falsifications], *Folha de São Paulo*, 20 April 1990, p. E–14).

31. Tzvetan Todorov, "Fictions et verités" [Fictions and truths], *L'Homme* 111–12 (1989): 9–10.

32. Dan Sperber, "Apparently Irrational Beliefs," in Martin Hollis and Steven Lukes, eds., *Rationality and Relativism* (Oxford: Basil Blackwell, 1982), p. 164.

33. Paul Veyne, *Did the Greeks Believe in Their Myths? An Essay on Constitutive Imagination* (Chicago: University of Chicago Press, 1988), pp. 83–84.

34. Roland Barthes, *Mythologies* (New York: Hill and Wang, 1972), p. 143.

35. Claude Lévi-Strauss, ed., *L'Identité* (Paris: Bernard Grasset, 1977), p. 332.

2. National and Regional Traditions in the Construction of Brazilian Identity

1. Barbara Weinstein, "Brazilian Regionalism," *Latin American Research Review* 17, no. 2 (1982): 275.

2. *República Velha* [Old Republic] is the name given to the period between the Proclamation of the Republic in 1889 and the Revolution of 1930.

3. See Ruben George Oliven, "State and Culture in Brazil," *Studies in Latin American Popular Culture*, vol. 5 (1986).

4. See Maria Isaura Pereira de Queiroz, "Cientistas sociais e autoconhecimento na cultura brasileira através do tempo" [Social scientists and self-knowledge in Brazilian culture through time], *Cadernos CERU*, no. 13 (1980).

5. Eduardo Jardim de Moraes, *A Brasilidade modernista* [Modernist Brazilian identity] (Rio de Janeiro: Graal, 1978), p. 105. [The term *brasilidade* has entered the North American academic discourse as a self-sense of "Brazilianness" that is expressed by Brazilian intellectuals and literary figures. More than

merely "Brazilian national identity," the term has come to mean the contradictory feelings of European versus African versus native traditions.—Trans.]

6. Eduardo Jardim de Moraes, *Brasilidade*, p. 52.

7. Mariza G. S. Peirano, *O antropólogo como cidadão: Louis Dumont e o
Caso Brasileiro* [The anthropologist as citizen: Louis Dumont and the Brazilian
case] (Brasilia: University of Brasilia Anthropology Series, 1984), no. 44.

8. See Mário de Andrade, *O turista aprendiz* [The apprentice tourist] (São
Paulo: Duas Cidades, 1983).

9. *Tenentista* refers to a nationalistic reform movement led by military men
at the rank of *tenente* [lieutenant]. *Tenentismo* was the name given to the ideology of the military movement led by the lieutenants in the armed forces cul-
minating with the 1930 Revolution.

10. For an account of the relationship between the state of São Paulo and
Brazil, see Simon Schwartzman, *São Paulo e o estado nacional* [São Paulo and
the nation-state] (São Paulo: DIFEL, 1975).

11. Joaquim Inojosa affirms that the *Regionalist Manifesto* was not published in 1926 but in 1952, the date when Gilberto Freyre probably would have
written it. See Joaquim Inojosa, *Pá de cal* [Concrete shovel] (Rio de Janeiro:
Meio-Dia, 1978). The author of the *Manifesto* affirms that the text was read in
1926 at the First Brazilian Congress on Regionalism that took place in Recife
and published in its first edition in 1952. See Gilberto Freyre. *Manifesto regionalista* (Recife: Instituto Joaquim Nabuco de Pesquisas Sociais, 1976), p. 52.

12. In a document written to celebrate the fiftieth anniversary of the
Manifesto, its author affirms that "while the Modern Art Week in São Paulo
and modernism in Rio . . . took great pride in . . . innovations, which are by the
way admirable, in erudite sectors of culture, . . . the movement in Recife, without excluding this kind of importation, also took upon itself, from the beginning, to research, reinterpret, and valorize inspirations from tellurian, traditional, oral, popular, and folkloric roots, some of which are anthropologically
intuitive, from the same culture. Everyday, spontaneous, rustic things rejected
by those in art or culture are sensitive to the fancy and erudite. Things seen as
uselessly archaic in the utilitarian arts, although some may be decorative like
furniture or home architecture, are already adapted to regional ecology and traditions. Further, the case of the art of lace making, embroidery, and sewing, and
the scandal, let us repeat, for the time when it appeared—the movement for the
art of cooking, cake making, candy making, and juice making with national
and regional fruits, the art of *batidas* [alcoholic drinks made from a sugar-based
Brazilian rum—*cachaça*—and fruit juices], almost all of it still made at home
but susceptible to industrialization without losing such intrinsic values,
rejected up to that time, of the homemade touch and taste" (Gilberto Freyre,
"O Movimento regionalista, tradicionalista e, a seu modo, modernista de
Recife" [Regionalist, traditionalist, and in its own way modernist movement
in Recife], in *Manifesto regionalista*, p. 28.)

13. Ibid., p. 54.

14. Ibid., p. 55.

15. Gilberto Freyre, "Brazilian Unity and Brazilian Regional Diversity," in
Brazil: An Interpretation (New York: Knopf, 1945), p. 67.

16. Ibid., p. 70.

17. Freyre, *Manifesto regionalista*, pp. 56–57.

18. Maria Isaura Pereira de Queiroz, "Do rural e do urbano no Brasil" [On rural and urban life in Brazil] in Tamás Szmercsányi and Oriowaldo Queda, eds., *Vida rural e mudança social* [Rural life and social change] (São Paulo: Nacional, 1973).

19. Roberto Schwarz, "As idéias fora do lugar" [Out of place ideas] in *Ao vencedor as batatas* [To the winner go the potatoes] (São Paulo: Duas Cidades, 1977).

20. Freyre, *Manifesto regionalista*, p. 59.

21. Ibid., pp. 72–73.

22. Ibid., p. 80.

23. Néstor Garcia Canclini, *Transforming Modernity: Popular Culture in Mexico* (Austin: University of Texas Press, 1993), p. 22.

24. Freyre, *Manifesto regionalista*, p. 76.

25. Renato Ortiz, *Cultura popular: Românticos e folcloristas* [Popular culture: Romantics and folklorists] (São Paulo: Graduate Program in Social Sciences, Catholic University, 1985), p. 11.

26. Renato Ortiz, "Cultura popular e memória nacional" [Popular culture and national collective memory] *Cadernos CERU*, no. 13 (1980): 13.

27. The "governors' policy" was a pact through which the presidency of the Republic alternated between the states of São Paulo and Minas Gerais. It also stipulated that the central government would not interfere in the internal affairs of each of the other states. The exchange policies at the time were designed to protect the price of coffee produced mainly in São Paulo. The 1930 Revolution that brought about the New Republic was a movement that originated because of the dissatisfaction on the part of the peripheral oligarchies. The Revolution bestowed leadership on Getúlio Vargas, a politician from the state of Rio Grande do Sul. He remained in power from 1930 until 1945 and was subsequently elected president from 1951 until 1954.

28. See Simon Schwartzman, Helena Maria Bousquet Bomeny, and Vanda Maria Ribeiro Costa, *Tempos de Capanema* [Capanema times] (Rio de Janeiro: Paz e Terra, 1984).

29. *Estado Novo* [New State] was the name given to the Getúlio Vargas dictatorship (1937–1945).

30. *Nova constituição da república dos Estados Unidos do Brasil* [New Constitution of the republic of the United States of Brazil], decreed on 10 November 1937 (São Paulo: Brasileira, 1937), p. 3.

31. *Intentona Comunista* was the name given to the failed armed insurrection carried out by the Communists with the objective of taking over power in 1935.

32. "As grandes demonstrações cívicas de hontem nesta capital. Homenagem à bandeira e à memória dos que tombaram em defesa do regimen, em 1935" [Yesterday's great civic demonstrations in this capital. Honors to the flag and to the memory of those who died in defense of the regime in 1935], *Correio da Manhã*, 27 November 1937.

33. The ISEB [Institute for Brazilian Advanced Studies] was a research entity created in 1955 by the federal government, and it was nationalistic in orientation. The CPC [Popular Center for Culture], linked to the National Union of Students, was created in 1962 and had as its objective the consciousness-raising of the masses through popular theater and other artistic forms. Both ended with the military coup of 1964.

34. *Superintendência do Desenvolvimtneto do Nordeste*, or "Agency for the Development of the Northeast," was a federal agency created during the 1950s to oversee and aid in the development of the Northeast.

35. Those who governed the states were called state presidents during the Old Republic. During the *Estado Novo*, they were appointed by the president of the Republic and were called "intervenors." During the greater part of the military regime (1964–1985) the governors were elected by the state legislative assemblies, but their names were indicated by the president of the Republic.

3. Rio Grande do Sul and Brazil: A Contradictory Relationship

1. Lourenço Mário Prunes, "O isolamento geográfico do Rio Grande do Sul" [Geographical isolation of Rio Grande do Sul], in *Fundamentos da cultura Rio Grandense* [Foundations of Rio Grandian culture] (Porto Alegre: Faculdade de Filosofia da Universidade do Rio Grande do Sul, 1962), Quinta série.

2. At the beginning of Brazilian colonization, the territory of Rio Grande do Sul was called Rio Grande de São Pedro; after 1760 the territory was called Captaincy of Rio Grande de São Pedro; and after independence, the name changed once more to Province of São Pedro. The territory was also known as the Continent of Rio Grande.

3. Sandra Jatahy Pesavento, *História do Rio Grande do Sul* [History of Rio Grande do Sul] (Porto Alegre: Mercado Aberto, 1980), p. 13.

4. These *Sesmarias* [land grants] were parcels of land measuring generally some three leagues by one league (thirteen thousand hectares) that were granted by the Portuguese Crown to whoever wished to cultivate them.

5. Erico Veríssimo, "Um romancista apresenta sua terra" [A novelist presents his land], in *Rio Grande do Sul: Terra e Povo* [Rio Grande do Sul: Land and people] (Porto Alegre: Globo, 1969), pp. 3–4.

6. Luiz Carlos Barbosa Lessa, *Os Doze Rio Grandes* [The twelve Rio Grandes] (Porto Alegre: SAMRIG, 1981). Thales de Azevedo mentions three areas in Rio Grande do Sul: the Gaúcho area, the colonial area, and the original Rio Grandian area. See *Gaúchos, notas de antropologia social* [Gaúchos, social anthropology notes] (Bahia: Tipografia Naval, 1943). See also "Rio Grande, imagem e consciência" [Rio Grande, image and consciousness], in *Os brasileiros: Estudos de "caráter nacional"* [Brazilians: Studies of "national character"] (Salvador: Universidade Federal da Bahia, 1981).

7. The word *guasca* seems to come from the Quechua word *huasca*, meaning string or rope. Today it means a kind of cord made from raw cowhide. *Guasca* was used to designate Rio Grandians because the abundance of cowhide in the state and the lack of other materials meant that Rio Grandians used cowhide for many different purposes. See Zeno Cardoso Nunes and Rui Cardoso Nunes, *Dicionário de regionalismos do Rio Grande do Sul* (Porto Alegre: Martins, 1982), pp. 237–40.

8. Augusto Meyer, *Gaúcho, história de uma palavra* [Gaúcho, history of a word] (Porto Alegre: Instituto Estadual do Livro, 1957).

9. For a similar process of creating symbols of national identity, see Ruben

George Oliven, "The Production and Consumption of Culture in Brazil," *Latin American Perspectives*, vol. 11, no. 1 (1984).

10. Flávio Loureiro Chaves, "O Gaúcho: Literatura e ideologia" [The Gaúcho: Literature and ideology], *O Estado de São Paulo*, vol. 4, no. 177 (30 October 1983): 2 (Suplemento "Cultura" [Culture supplement]).

11. *Pampa* is the name given to the vast plains of the Gaúcho campanha as well as the similar region in Argentina and Uruguay whose natural pasture lands are ideal for raising cattle. For an analysis of the Euro-American ranching complex, see Arnold Strickon, "The Euro-American Ranching Complex," in Anthony Leeds and Andrew P. Vayda, eds., *Man, Culture, and Animals: The Role of Animals in Human Ecological Adjustments* (Washington, D.C.: American Association for the Advancement of Science, 1965), no. 78. For an analysis of the identity of present-day Gaúcho peons who live in the frontier region between Uruguay and Brazil, see Ondina Fachel Leal, "The Gaúchos: Male Culture and Identity in the Pampas," doctoral dissertation in anthropology, University of California, Berkeley, 1989).

12. Francisco José Oliveira Vianna, *Populações meridionais do Brasil* [Southern populations in Brazil], vol. 2: *O campeador Rio Grandense* [The Rio Grandian fieldhand] (Rio de Janeiro: Paz e Terra, 1974), pp. 159, 168–69, 195–96, and 199–200. The first edition of the second volume of this book was published posthumously in 1952, although, according to the publishers, it was already "finished" at the end of the 1920s. The idea of the ease of obtaining the means of subsistence is responsible for what a contemporary historian has called the "myth of workless production." See Décio Freitas, "O Gaúcho: O mito da 'produção sem trabalho' " [Gaúcho: Myth of workless production], in José H. Dacanal and Sergius Gonzaga, *RS: Cultura e ideologia* [Rio Grande do Sul: Culture and ideology] (Porto Alegre: Mercado Aberto, 1980).

13. Auguste Saint-Hilaire, *Viagem ao Rio Grande do Sul* [Travel to Rio Grande do Sul] (Belo Horizonte: Itatiaia, 1974), p. 47. Dreys concurred with this statement when he said that "in the ranches, the black has little to do except on the occasion of round-ups." See Nicolau Dreys, Notícia descriptiva da província do Rio Grande de São Pedro do Sul [Descriptive note about the province of Rio Grande de São Pedro do Sul] (Rio de Janeiro: J. Villeneuve, 1839), p. 203.

14. Saint-Hilaire, *Viagem ao Rio Grande do Sul*, p. 73.

15. Fernando Henrique Cardoso, *Capitalismo e escravidão no Brasil meridional* [Capitalism and slavery in southern Brazil] (Rio de Janeiro: Paz e Terra, 1977), p. 115.

16. Ibid., p. 81. See also Mário José Maestri Filho, *O escravo no Rio Grande do Sul. A Charqueada e a Gênese do Escravo Gaúcho* [The slave in Rio Grande do Sul. Beef jerky processing and the genesis of the Gaúcho slave] (Caxias do Sul: EDUCS, 1984).

17. Spencer L. Leitman, "Negros Farrapos: Hipocrisia racial no sul do Brasil no século XIX" [Blacks in rags: Racial hypocrisy in southern Brazil in the nineteenth century], in José Hildebrando Dacanal, ed., *A Revolução Farroupilha: História e interpretação* [Farroupilha revolution: History and interpretation] (Porto Alegre: Mercado Aberto, 1985), p. 65.

18. Margaret Marchiori Bakos, "A escravidão negra e os farroupilhas" [Black slavery and the Farroupilhas], in Dacanal, *A revolução farroupilha*, pp. 79, 94.

19. *Bandeirantes* [flag bearers] were members of *bandeiras* [flags], the name given to expeditions that between the end of the sixteenth century and the beginning of the eighteenth went from the captaincy of São Vicente and later from São Paulo toward the backlands to enslave Indians and to search for precious stones.

20. See, among others, Balduíno Rambo, "A Fisionomia do Rio Grande do Sul" [The face of Rio Grande do Sul], in *Fundamentos da Cultura Rio Grandense* [Foundations of Rio Grandian culture] (Porto Alegre: Faculdade de Filosofia da Universidade do Rio Grande do Sul, 1954), Primeira série; Othelo Rosa, "Formação do Rio Grande do Sul" [Formation of Rio Grande do Sul], in *Fundamentos da cultura Rio-Grandense* [Foundations of Rio Grandian culture] (Porto Alegre: Faculdade de Filosofia da Universidade do Rio Grande do Sul, 1957), Segunda série; Luís Gonzaga, "O Indio no Rio Grande do Sul" [Indian in Rio Grande do Sul], in *Primeiro seminário de estudos gaúchos* [First seminar on Gaúcho studies] (Porto Alegre: Pontifícia Universidade Católica do Rio Grande do Sul, 1957); Pedro Ignácio Schmitz, "Informações elementares sobre a influência indígena na formação do Rio Grande do Sul" [Elementary information about the indigenous influence in the formation of Rio Grande do Sul], in *O Indio no Rio Grande do Sul—Aspectos arqueológicos, históricos, etnográficos e étnicos* [The Indian in Rio Grande do Sul—archaeological, historical, ethnographic, and ethnic aspects] (Porto Alegre: Governo do Estado do Rio Grande do Sul [Comissão Executiva de Homenagem ao Indio, Biênio da Colonização e Imigração], 1975).

21. Moysés Vellinho, *Capitania d'El-Rei* (Porto Alegre: Globo, 1964), pp. 88, 175, 176.

22. José Hildebrando Dacanal, "A miscigenação que não houve" [The miscegenation that never occurred], in Dacanal and Gonzaga, *RS: Cultura e ideologia*, pp. 30–31, 32.

23. Ligia Chiappini Moraes Leite, *No entretanto dos tempos: Literatura e história em João Simões Lopes Neto* [In the meanwhile of time: Literature and history in João Simões Lopes Neto] (São Paulo: Martins Fontes, 1988), p. 148.

24. Jorge Salis Goulart, A formação do Rio Grande do Sul [The formation of Rio Grande do Sul] (Porto Alegre: Martins Livreiro, 1985), pp. 108–9.

25. Concerning the conflicts in Rio Grande do Sul, see José do Patrocínio Motta, *República fratricida. Revoluções Rio Grandense de 1835–1932* [Fratricidal republic. Rio Grandian revolutions, 1835–1932] (Porto Alegre: Martins Livreiro, 1989).

26. Joseph L. Love, *Rio Grande do Sul and Brazilian Regionalism, 1882–1930* (Stanford: Stanford University Press, 1971), p. 72.

27. Carlos Reverbel, *Maragatos e Pica-Paus: Guerra civil e degola no Rio Grande* [Maragatos (the term used to designate those who fought against the Republicans who were in power in Rio Grande do Sul) and Pica-Paus (the term used to designate Rio Grande Republicans): civil war and beheading in Rio Grande] (Porto Alegre: L&PM, 1985), p. 52.

28. For information on the socioeconomic reasons for the Farroupilha Revolution, see Spencer Lewis Leitman, *Raízes Sócio-econômicas da guerra dos Farrapos: Um capítulo da história do Brasil no século XIX* [Socioeconomic roots of the Farrapos war: A chapter in nineteenth-century Brazilian history] (Rio de Janeiro: Graal, 1979).

29. *Farrapo,* or its diminutive *farroupilha,* means an old or torn rag, and it was a pejorative nickname that the legalist imperial troops gave to the Rio Grandian rebels because of the miserable state of their clothing. The revolutionaries adopted the nickname as a term of honor and the revolution entered the pages of history as the Farroupilha Revolution with the rebels being the *farrapos.*

30. Moysés Vellinho, "O Rio Grande e o Prata: Contrastes" [The Rio Grande and the Prata: Contrasts], in Vellinho, *Capitania D'El-Rei,* p. 217.

31. Rubens de Barcellos, "A ideologia separatista e o caráter rio-grandense" [Separatist ideology and the Rio Grandian character], in *Estudos Rio Grandenses* [Rio Grandian studies] (Porto Alegre: Globo, 1955), p. 48.

32. Vellinho, *Capitania,* p. 239.

33. Victor Russomano, A revolução dos farrapos [Ragamuffin revolution] (Rio de Janeiro: Oficina Gráfica da Secretaria Geral de Educação e Cultura, 1935), pp. 24, 30, 34.

34. Concerning the Rio Grande do Sul flag, see Walter Spalding, "Bandeira, Brasão e Hino Rio Grandenses" [Rio Grandian flag, coat of arms, and anthem], *Boletim da DAER do Rio Grande do Sul* 18, no. 69 (1955).

35. Vellinho, *Capitania,* p. 239.

36. Ligia Chiappini Moraes Leite, *Regionalismo e Modernismo (O "Caso" Gaúcho)* [Regionalism and Modernism (The Gaúcho "Case")] (São Paulo: Atica, 1979), p. 175.

37. Ibid., p. 170.

38. Pedro Simon, "Marginalização política do Rio Grande" [Political marginalization of Rio Grande], *Zero Hora,* 20 September 1985, p. 22 (Suplemento "Farrapos").

39. At the beginning of the 1960s, a journalist published a series of articles in the Rio de Janeiro newspaper, *Correio da Manhã* (later collected in a book) in which he denounced the impoverishment of Rio Grande do Sul and concluded that "RGS is not in any condition to recompose itself alone from the bloodletting that was imposed on it be the federal government" (Franklin Oliveira, *Rio Grande do Sul: Um novo nordeste* [RGS: A new northeast] (Rio de Janeiro: Civilização Brasileira, 1961), p. 200.

40. Pedro Silveira Bandeira, "Os problemas do Rio Grande," *Diário do Sul* (31 October and 1 November 1987): 2. Concerning the economic characteristics of Rio Grande do Sul in relation to the rest of Brazil, see Pedro Fernando Cunha de Almeida, ed., *A economia gaúcha e os anos 80: Uma trajetória regional no contexto da crise brasileira* [Gaúcho economy and the eighties: A regional trajectory in the context of the Brazilian crisis], 3 vols. (Porto Alegre: Fundação de Economia e Estatística, 1990).

41. "Cavalarianos dizem que batalha continua" [Horsemen say that the battle continues], *Zero Hora,* 29 May 1985, p. 30.

42. Sérgio da Costa Franco, "Um fiasco," *Zero Hora,* 23 March 1985, p. 2.

43. Jarbas Lima, "Carta aos libertadores" [Letter to the liberators], *Zero Hora* (10 June 1984), p. 7 (italics added).

44. Leonid Streliaev, "Por uma república gaúcha," *Veja* 20, no. 5 (3 February 1988): 90.

45. "Surge o Partido da República Farroupilha," *Zero Hora,* 30 May 1990.

46. Jarbas Passarinho, "O separatismo gaúcho" [Gaúcho separatism], *Folha de São Paulo*, 7 June 1990, p. A–3.

47. Irton Marx, *Vai nascer um novo país: República do Pampa Gaúcho. União dos estados de Santa Catarina e Rio Grande do Sul* [A new country is about to be born: The republic of the Gaúcho pampa. Union of the states of Santa Catarina and Rio Grande do Sul] (Santa Cruz do Sul: Excelsior, 1990). In 1986 a book had already been published discussing the independence of the three southern states in Brazil. See Sérgio Alves Oliveira, *Independência do Sul* [Southern independence] (Porto Alegre: Martins Livreiro, 1986).

48. Marx, *Vai nascer*, pp. 188, 185.

49. *Zero Hora*, 30 May 1985, p. 2; *Zero Hora*, 22 December 1985, p. 2; *ISTO É*, 5 February 1986, pp. 16–23.

50. *Zero Hora*, 15 February 1986, p. 4; *Zero Hora*, 16 March 1986, p. 11; *Diário do Sul*, 28 August 1987, p. 2.

51. Elio Falcão Vieira, *Zero Hora*, 8 May 1985, p. 4, and 18 February 1986, p. 4.

4. In Search of a Lost Time: The Gaúcho Traditionalist Movement

1. Glauco Carneiro, *Lusardo, o ultimo caudilho* [Lusardo, the last caudilho] (Rio de Janeiro: Nova Fronteira, 1977), p. 40.

2. Rogério Haesbaert da Costa, *RS: Latifúndio e identidade regional* [RS: Latifundia and regional identity] (Porto Alegre: Mercado Aberto, 1988), p. 36.

3. Sérgio da Costa Franco, "A Campanha," in *Rio Grande do Sul: Terra e povo* [Rio Grande do Sul: Land and people] (Porto Alegre: Globo, 1969), pp. 65–66. Reviewing his article, Franco affirmed that "the great problem in the southern zone was the awful distribution of wealth generated by the long predominance of the pastoral latifundia. Capital concentrated in huge cattle farms does not multiply initiatives nor does it stimulate parallel investments. This was evidenced in the southern *Campanha* which was able to stem its regression only because of the advent of mechanized rice industry and the establishment, in the Pelotas region, of some farm colonies. These two elements stimulated the beginning of industry and a certain diversification of activities. The municipalities that remained pastoral only are alarmingly underdeveloped" (Sérgio da Costa Franco, "Zona Sul," *Zero Hora*, 1 August 1989, p. 2). Today, data show that this picture is even more pronounced. A study carried out by the Department of Planning for the state of Rio Grande do Sul demonstrated that "in 1939, the region around Bagé [one of the main municipalities of the *Campanha*] was responsible for 4 percent of the Gaúcho gross product. This percentage fell to 2 percent in 1980. . . . The Uruguaiana region [another of the main municipalities in the *Campanha*], which provided 7 percent of the Gaúcho GIP [Gross Internal Product] in 1939, provided only 4 percent in 1980. . . . The per capita income follows the same pattern: in Bagé, it was 20 percent greater than the state average in 1939. In 1980 it was 19 percent below average. . . . In Uruguaiana, the situation was not much different: from 13 percent above average in 1939 to 12 percent below average in 1980. . . . The document from the Planning Department detects more dark clouds in the southern region when it predicts that in the period from 1980 to 2022, Rio Grande do Sul will have an annual average growth of 4.4 percent. In the Bagé

region, however, the growth will not be above 3.5 percent, and in the Uruguaiana region it will not surpass 3.8 percent. On the other hand, it is expected that the region around Caxias do Sul [a municipality of Italian colonization located in the northeastern part of the state] will have, during the same period, a growth of 6.1 percent. The per capita income, which was 30 percent below average in 1939, in 1980 was already 35 percent above average, and in 2022 it will be an alarming 163 percent above average. Everything comes from the participation in the Gaúcho GIP of 5 percent in 1939 to 8 percent in 1980 and, according to projections, to 12 percent in 2011" (José Francisco Shuster, "O norte avança, o sul recua" [The north advances, the south retreats], *Zero Hora*, 22 July 1989, p. 37.

4. In 1990 a movement appeared in the hope of creating the state of Piratini (the capital of the Rio Grandian Republic proclaimed through the Farroupilha Revolution) which would comprise 70 percent of the present-day state of Rio Grande do Sul. A legislative action was presented to obtain legal authorization to conduct a plebiscite consulting the inhabitants of the southern region of the state about the idea. The action was considered unconstitutional by the Commission on the Constitution and Justice of the House of Representatives, causing it to be tabled. The movement was led by the former mayor (and, on the occasion of the proposal, a federal representative) from Pelotas, a city located in the south of Rio Grande do Sul and one of the richest cities in the state during the time of the meat-drying processing. Today the city is in stagnation. Recognizing that "the region missed a step in history when it did not substitute meat-drying processes for refrigeration, 'the argumentation points to the fact that the precarious political influence of the region is characterized by the composition of its representation in the Legislative Assembly and in Congress: of the fifty-five state representatives, only eight belong to the lower half of the state whereas in the Federal Chamber, there are twenty-seven representatives from the North and four from the South' " (Marcelo Rech, "Estado de Piratini, idéia para retomar crescimento da Zona Sul," [Piratini state, idea for reestablishing growth in the southern zone], *Zero Hora* (22 April 1990), p. 12.

5. See Cyro Martins, *Sem rumo* [Aimless] (Rio de Janeiro: Ariel, 1937); *Porteira fechada* [Closed gate] (Porto Alegre: Globo, 1944); *Estrada nova* [New road] (São Paulo: Brasiliense, 1954).

6. Sergius Gonzaga, "As mentiras sobre of Gaúcho: Primeiras contribuições da literatura" [Lies about the Gaúcho: First contributions to literature], in José Hildebrando Dacanal and Sergius Gonzaga, eds., *RS: Cultura e Ideologia* [RS: Culture and ideology] (Porto Alegre: Mercado Aberto, 1980), pp. 125–26.

7. João Cezimbra Jacques, *Assuntos do Rio Grande do Sul* [Rio Grande do Sul subjects] (Porto Alegre: Erus, 1979), pp. 56, 58.

8. Celi Regina J. Pinto, *Positivismo: Um projeto político alternativo (RS: 1889–1930)* [Positivism: An alternative political project (RS: 1889–1930)] (Porto Alegre: L&PM, 1986), p. 36.

9. Tau Golin points to the creation, also at the beginning of the century, of the associations in Santa Cruz and in Encruzilhada, which generally are not cited by the traditionalists. See his book *A Ideologia do Gauchismo* [Gauchism ideology] (Porto Alegre: Tchê, 1983), pp. 32–33.

10. The word *crioulo* in Rio Grande do Sul connotes what is native of any part of the state, and therefore pure and original.

11. From an interview with Luiz Carlos Barbosa Lessa on 4 October 1983.

12. In that same interview with Barbosa Lessa on 4 October 1983, he affirms that, in 1948, "to see eight young men in downtown Porto Alegre, dressed in Gaúcho fashion, would cause as great an impact as if today one saw a flying saucer go down on the Praça da Alfândega and a group of Martians came out" (Presentation at the seminar, "Sociedade e Cultura no Rio Grande do Sul" [Culture and society in Rio Grande do Sul], in the Graduate Program in Social Anthropology at the Federal University of Rio Grande do Sul, on 18 June 1985).

13. Antônio Augusto Fagundes, "A Verdadeira História do Tradicionalismo" [The true story of traditionalism], in Cyro Dutra Ferreira, ed., *35 CTG: O Pioneiro do Movimento Tradicionalista Gaúcho—MTG* [35 CTG: The pioneer of the Gaúcho traditionalist movement—GTM] (Porto Alegre: Martins Livreiro, 1987), p. 13.

14. The word *nativism* has different meanings in English and in Portuguese. In Rio Grande do Sul, it is used in reference to the movements that valorize and praise what is considered "native" to the state.

15. Luiz Carlos Barbosa Lessa, *Nativismo: Um fenômeno social gaúcho* [Nativism: A Gaúcho social phenomenon] (Porto Alegre: L&PM, 1985), pp. 56–57.

16. See Gerson Moura, *Tio Sam chega ao Brazil. A Penetração cultural americana* [Uncle Sam arrives in Brazil. American Cultural Penetration] (São Paulo: Brasiliense, 1984).

17. "The Gaúcho bunkhouse in the frontier was a rustic construction of average size with a thatched roof, made of small wooden planks in the Mountain Fields. In general, the flooring, when it existed, was made of rough wood; otherwise it was a dirt floor. The structure did not have doors and, at times, one of the walls was missing where the bonfire would be lit. The structure serves as a shelter and nurturing place for servants and itinerant horsemen, travelers, muleteers, or vagrants. In this structure the traditional barbecue is prepared and eaten, the Chimarrão is drunk, and during free times improvised meetings are held around the bonfire. These meetings contribute to the democratic participation of bosses and servants, travelers, peons, muleteers, cart drivers, and vagrants, all of whom tell tales of war, of their cattle herding, of wagon trains, of field services, of hunting, fishing, and love. At the same time the group drinks a little moonshine, someone plays the accordion, someone strums a guitar, and they sing traditional songs or recite traditional poems" (Zeno Cardoso Nunes and Rui Cardoso Nunes, *Dicionário de Regionalismos do Rio Grande Do Sul* [Dictionary of Rio Grandian regionalism] (Porto Alegre: Martins Livreiro, 1982), pp. 203–4].

18. Presentation by Luiz Carlos Barbosa Lessa on 18 June 1985, and Barbosa Lessa, *Nativism*, p. 58.

19. Hélio Moro Mariante, *História do Tradicionalismo Gaúcho* [History of Gaúcho traditionalism], Porto Alegre, Fundação Instituto Gaúcho de Tradição e Folclore, *Cadernos Gaúchos*, no. 1 (1976): p. 11.

20. Barbosa Lessa, *Nativism*, p. 64.

21. Interview with Luiz Carlos Barbosa Lessa on 4 October 1983.

22. Barbosa Lessa, *Nativism*, p. 75.

23. Presentation by Barbosa Lessa on 18 June 1985.

24. For a list of the founders of the '35 CTG, see the book by one of them: Cyro Dutra Ferreira, *35 CTG: O Pioneiro do Movimento Tradicionalista Gaúcho–MTG* [35 CTG: The pioneer in the Gaúcho Traditionalist Movement–GTM] (Porto Alegre: Martins Livreiro, 1987), pp. 37–38.

25. *Fifth Column* is a term that originated during the Spanish Civil War (1936–39) when Franco claimed that he had five "columns" with which to attack Madrid, the fifth being the people who were inside the city and who would join him when he attacked. The term is used often in Portuguese.

26. André Luiz Jacobus, *A questão étnica como fonte de tradicionalismo* [The ethnic question as the source of traditionalism], Final paper presented in the course "Society and Culture in Rio Grande do Sul," Graduate Program in Social Anthropology at the Federal University of Rio Grande do Sul, 1983, pp. 2–3.

27. Sérgio Alves Teixeira, *Os recados das festas: Representações e poder no Brasil* [The messages of the festas: Representations and power in Brazil] (Rio de Janeiro: FUNARTE, 1988), p. 54.

28. About the German colonization, see Jean Roche, *A colonização alemã e o Rio Grande do Sul* [German colonization and Rio Grande do Sul] (Porto Alegre: Globo, 1969), and Emílio Willems, *A aculturação dos alemães no Brasil: Estudo antropológico dos imigrantes alemães e seus descendentes no Brasil* [German acculturation in Brazil: Anthropological study of German immigrants and their descendants in Brazil] (São Paulo: Editora Nacional, 1946). About the Italian immigration in Rio Grande do Sul, see Thales Azevedo, *Italianos e Gaúchos: Os anos pioneiros da colonização italiana no Rio Grande do Sul* [Italians and Gaúchos: The pioneer years of Italian colonization in Rio Grande do Sul] (Porto Alegre: A Nação, 1975). About the Gaúcho and his horse, see Emílio Willems, *Acculturation and the Horse Complex among German-Brazilians,"* American Anthropologist, *vol. 46 (1944), and Roger Bastide, "O cavalo e o pampa" [The horse and the pampas], in Brasil: Terra de contrastes* [Brazil: Land of contrasts] (São Paulo: DIFEL, 1964).

29. From 1955, when the Italian immigrants to Rio Grande do Sul were celebrating their eightieth year, until 1979, there were six governors of the state with Italian surnames.

30. Ralph Linton, *The Study of Man: An Introduction* (New York: Appleton-Century, 1966); Donald Pierson, *Teoria e pesquisa em sociologia* [Theory and research in sociology] (São Paulo: Melhoramentos, 1968). About the influence of Donald Pierson in Brazil, see Lúcia Lippi de Oliveira, "Donald Pierson e a sociologia no Brasil" [Donald Pierson and Brazilian sociology], *Boletim Informativo e Bibliográfico de Ciências Sociais*, no. 23 (1987).

31. Interview with Luiz Carlos Barbosa Lessa on 4 October 1983.

32. Luiz Carlos Barbosa Lessa, *O sentido e o valor do tradicionalismo* [Meaning and value of traditionalism] (Porto Alegre: SAMRIG, 1979), p. 5.

33. About this subject see Ruben George Oliven, "A Cidade como categoria sociológica" [The city as a sociological category], in *Urbanização e mudança social no Brasil* [Urbanization and social change in Brazil] (Petrópolis: Vozes, 1988).

34. Barbosa Lessa, *Value and Meaning*, pp. 7–8.

35. These Roman Catholic festivals involve intense popular participation and celebrate, respectively, the Divine Holy Spirit and the Virgin of the Navigators.

36. Barbosa Lessa, *Value and Meaning*, p. 8.

37. Interview with Antônio Augusto Fagundes on 14 September 1981.

38. Glaucus Saraiva, *Manual do Tradicionalista: Orientação geral para tradicionalistas e centros de tradições gaúchas* [Traditionalist manual: General orientation for traditionalists and centers for Gaúcho traditions] (Porto Alegre: Sulina, 1968).

39. Mariante, *History*, p. 13.

40. The *carreteiro* is a simple dish made with rice and chopped beef jerky, and it was the traditional meal of the Gaúcho troopers. Similar to what happened to the *feijoada* (a dish prepared primarily with black beans and leftover pork), which from being a slave dish became a symbol of Brazilian national identity, the *carreteiro* became a symbol of Gaúcho identity (about *feijoada* see Peter Fry, "Feijoada e Soul Food: Notas sobre a manipulação de símbolos étnicos e nacionais" [Feijoada and soul food: Notes about the manipulation of ethnic and national symbols], in *Para Inglês Ver: Identidade e Política na Cultura Brasileira* [For the English to see: Identity and politics in Brazilian Culture] (Rio de Janeiro: Zahar, 1982).

41. *Pólos culturais do Rio Grande do Sul* [Cultural poles in Rio Grande do Sul] (Porto Alegre: Secretaria de Cultura Desporto e Turismo do Rio Grande do Sul, n.d. [1979–1983]).

42. About the conflicts that this policy generated with other sectors, like the theater and plastic arts, see Ruben George Oliven, "A fabricação do Gaúcho" [The manufacturing of the Gaúcho], in *Ciências Sociais Hoje—1984 (Anuário de Antropologia, Política, e Sociologia)* [Social sciences today—1984 (anthropology, political science, and sociology annual] (São Paulo: Cortez, 1984).

43. The word *California*, in Brazil, stands for a fortune or a source of wealth. In Rio Grande do Sul, the term is used to designate horse races that have more than two participants, and to designate some of the wartime invasions that some of the inhabitants of the state conducted in Uruguay in the middle of the last century.

44. See Rosângela Araujo, "Sob o signo da canção: Uma análise de festivais nativistas do Rio Grande do Sul" [Under the sign of the song: An analysis of nativist festivals in Rio Grande do Sul], Porto Alegre, Federal University of Rio Grande do Sul, Master's Thesis, 1987.

45. See Oliven, "Manufacturing."

46. Barbosa Lessa, *Nativism*, p. 98.

47. Mariante, *History*, p. 12.

48. Introduction to the new edition of *Meaning and Value of Traditionalism*, p. 4.

49. *Zero Hora*, 22 June 1986, and *Zero Hora*, special twenty-fifth anniversary supplement, 4 May 1989, p. 86.

50. *Diário do Sul*, 24 June 1988.

51. See João Fábio Caminoto, "A Nação Gaúcha" [The Gaúcho nation], *Veja* (14 September 1994): 68–69.

52. Interview with Antônio Augusto Fagundes on 14 September 1981.

53. Keeping in mind the two symbolic differences in the processes, this process has a certain similarity to that described by Yvonne Maggie Alves Velho for the *terreiros* in Rio de Janeiro. See her book, *Guerra de Orixá: Um*

estudo de ritual e conflito [War of the gods: A study of ritual and conflict] (Rio de Janeiro: Zahar, 1977).

54. See José Vicente Tavares dos Santos, *Matuchos: exclusão e luta. Do Sul para a Amazônia* [Matuchos: Exclusion and struggle. From the South to Amazonia] (Petrópolis: Vozes, 1993).

55. See João Fábio Caminoto, "A Nação Gaúcha" [The Gaúcho nation], *Veja* (14 September 1994): 68.

56. Lélia Pereira da Silva Nunes, "Gaúcho Traditionalist Movement in Santa Catarina," paper presented in the workshop "Sociology of Brazilian Culture," at the Eleventh Annual Meeting of the National Association of Graduate Studies in the Social Sciences, Aguas de São Pedro, São Paulo, 1987, p. 2.

57. Arthur Tramujas Neto, "Passe a cuia, chê!" [Pass the gourd, partner], *Leite Quente* 1, no. 2 (1989): 25.

58. Antônio Augusto Fagundes, "Confederação: Comissão examina o assunto" [Federation: Commission examines the matter], *Zero Hora: Guia*, 15 October 1988, p. 12.

59. See Caminoto, *Gaúcho Nation*, p. 68.

60. In November 1988, in La Plata, Argentina, the Permanent International Coordinating Commission of Gaúcho Tradition (composed of Argentines, Brazilians, and Uruguayans) sponsored the Fourth International Congress on Gaúcho Tradition during which the geographical area of Gaúcho culture was defined: "Thus we came to the configuration of a circle that takes as a referential diameter the 30th latitude parallel South, going through Mendoza (southeastern reference in Argentina) and a bit beyond Sorocaba (northeastern reference in Brazil). In this immense area, one observes the gathering of autochthonous American traditions that have as a common element the Guarani ritual of the *chimarrão—mate* tea drunk from a gourd through a silver straw (a tradition that does not exist in any other part of our planet) and as the objective, a greater universal friendship. This definition was adopted by the Thirty-fourth Traditionalist Congress o Rio Grande do Sul, which took place in Caçapava do Sul in January 1989" (Luiz Carlos Barbosa Lessa, *O Cevador* [The person who pours the water and serves the *mate* tea], proposition presented and approved in the First State Congress on Culture, Porto Alegre, 1989).

5. The Social Construction of the Gaúcho Identity

1. Rogério Mendelski, "Regionalismo não Resiste à Invasão das Discotecas" [Regionalism does not resist the invasion of discotheques], *Folha da Manhã* (31 December 1979): 21. The Piratini village, located in the southern part of the state was the first capital of the Rio Grandian Republic proclaimed by the Farroupilhas. The Republic was also designated the Piratini Republic.

2. Rosângela Araújo, "Sob o Signo da Canção: Uma análise de festivais de nativistas do Rio Grande do Sul" [Under the sign of the song: An analysis of Gaúcho festivals in Rio Grande do Sul], Porto Alegre, masters thesis in social anthropology, Federal University of Rio Grande do Sul, 1987. The president of the Gaúcho Association of Musical Events affirmed, during the First Congress of Gaúcho Music Promoters, that in 1988 "the average attendance at each of the fifty festivals was around 5,000 people. This means a total of

some 900,000 people were reached, counting only the presentations in schools or theaters, plus approximately 500,000 in the camps" (*Zero Hora*, "Gaúcho Festivals: A Larger Public Than at Soccer Matches," 12 July 1989, Second Notebook, p. 6).

3. We are speaking of Rádio Liberdade FM [FM Liberty radio], which was honored for being the "Communication Vehicle of the Year" in 1989 by the Rio-Grandian Propaganda Association. See Luiz Fonseca and Tude Munhoz, "Délvio Olvedo, fé no nativismo, espaço total na LIBERDADE," [Délvio Olvedo, faith in native culture, total space in Liberty radio], Tarca, *Cultura Gaúcha* 2, no. 9 (1985).

4. See Nilda Aparecida Jacks, "Mídia nativa" [Native media], masters thesis, University of São Paulo, School of Communications, 1987.

5. See Maria Eunice de Souza Maciel, "Bailões, é disto que o povo gosta" [Folk dances, this is what people like], masters thesis in social anthropology, Federal University of Rio Grande do Sul, Porto Alegre, 1984.

6. In 1980, 28.65 percent of the economically active population in Rio Grande do Sul was concentrated in the primary sector (cattle activities, agriculture, and fishing), 25.77 percent in the secondary sector (industry), and 45.58 percent in the tertiary sector (services, commerce, social activities, public administration, transportation, and communications). See *Resenha estatística do Rio Grande So Sul* (Porto Alegre: Fundação de Economia e Estatística, 1985), p. 11. It is estimated that by the year 2020, Rio Grande do Sul will have 11 million inhabitants and that 95 percent of its population will live in urban centers. See "Aumenta número de gaúchos que saem do campo para a cidade" [The number of Gaúchos who leave the country for the city increases] *Zero Hora*, 28 January 1989, p. 26.

7. The "whitest" state in Brazil is Santa Catarina, where 91.44 percent of the population declares itself white. See *Censo demográfico: dados gerais, migração, instrução, fecundidade, mortalidade (IX Recenseamento geral do Brasil, 1980)* [Demographic census: General data, migration, instruction, birthrate, mortality (ninth general census in Brazil, 1980] (Rio de Janeiro: Fundação Instituto Brasileiro de Geografia e Estatística, 1983), pp. 34–35.

8. Renato Ortiz, *Cultura brasileira e identidade nacional* [Brazilian culture and national identity] (São Paulo: Brasiliense, 1985), p. 41.

9. Beatriz Góis Dantas, *Vovô nagô e papai branco: Usos e abusos da Africa no Brasil* [Nagô granddaddy and white daddy: Uses and abuses of Africa in Brazil] (Rio de Janeiro: Graal, 1988), p. 151.

10. João Simões Lopes Neto, *Lendas do sul* [Southern legends] (Porto Alegre: Globo, 1980), p. 87. About the legend of the Little Black Boy, see Lígia Chiappini Moraes Leite, *No entretanto dos tempos: Literatura e história em João Simões Lopes Neto* [In the meanwhile of times: Literature and history in João Simões Lopes Neto] (São Paulo: Martins Fontes, 1987).

11. Augusto Meyer, *Prosa do Pago* [Prose of the homeland] (Rio de Janeiro: São José, 1960), p. 106.

12. Ari Pedro Oro, "Immigrants Européens et Religions Afro-Brésiliennes dans le Sud du Brésil" [European immigrants and Afro-Brazilian religions in the south of Brazil] *Archives de Sciences Sociales des Religions*, no. 68/1 (1989).

13. Ibid.; "Negros e brancos nas religiões afro-brasileiras no Rio Grande do

Sul" [Blacks and whites in the Afro-Brazilian religions in Rio Grande do Sul] Comunicações do ISER, no. 28 (1988), pp. 36, 45.

14. Rosa argues that although there may have been little miscegenation of whites and Indians in Rio Grande do Sul, the Indian's influence "cannot be recognized only through a morphologic aspect. More important is the psychological aspect; no doubt something of it remained in our soul. There was a transmission of habits and customs, primarily those from the minuanos and charruas. For example, one always cites the use of *boleadeiras* [The dictionary of Rio Grandian regionalism defines this word as "an instrument used by field hands to capture animals and used during wars to bring down the enemy. It has three round stones covered with leather and linked by laced cord called *soga*" (p. 69)]. It seems to me, however, that pride and a sense of freedom, both characteristics of the Gaúcho, were precious gifts from our horsemen Indians." For Rosa, although the Indians may appear in such a small number, they contributed to the character of the Gaúcho as far as horsemanship was concerned, and through their pride and desire for freedom (Othelo Rosa, "Formação do Rio Grande do Sul" [Formation of Rio Grande do Sul], *Fundamentos da Cultura Rio-Grandense* [Foundations of Rio Grandian culture], Segunda série (Porto Alegre: Faculdade de Filosofia da Universidade do Rio Grande do Sul, 1957), p. 20).

15. See "Princesa do carnaval devolve a faixa" [Carnival princess returns her sash], *Zero Hora* (8 December 1988), p. 38.

16. See Demosthenes Gonzalez, *Roteiro de um boêmio* [A bohemian's logbook] (Porto Alegre: Sulina, 1986), pp. 34–36.

17. Thales de Azevedo, *Carta para Ruben George Oliven* [Letter to Ruben George Oliven] (Salvador, 4 June 1984).

18. Mary Douglas, *Purity and Danger: An Analysis of the Concepts of Pollution and Taboo*. New York: Praeger, 1966.

19. Introduction in the newspaper *A tradição* [Tradition] to the *Carta do Seival* [Letter from the field], no 1 (1981): 4.

20. Ibid., pp. 7, 30.

21. J. C. Paixão Côrtes, *Falando em Tradição e Folclore Gaúcho: Excertos jornalísticos* [Speaking of Gaúcho folklore and tradition: Newspaper clippings] (Porto Alegre: Sultepa, 1981), p. 23.

22. For an example of a careful survey of Gaúcho folklore, see João Simões Lopes Neto, *Cancioneiro Guasca* (Porto Alegre: Globo, 1960) [originally published in 1910].

23. Luiz Carlos Barbosa Lessa, *Nativismo: Um Fenômeno social gaúcho* [Nativism: A Gaúcho social phenomenon] (Porto Alegre: L&PM, 1985), pp. 71–72.

24. Augusto Meyer, *Cancioneiro Gaúcho* [Gaúcho songbook] (Porto Alegre: Globo, 1952), p. 23.

25. João Cezimbra Jacques, *Ensaio sobre os costumes do Rio Grande do Sul* [Essay on Rio Grandian customs] (Porto Alegre: ERUS, 1979), p. 75.

26. See Mikhail Bakhtin, *Rabelais and His World* (Bloomington: Indiana University Press, 1984); Carlo Ginzburg, *The Cheese and the Worms: The Cosmos of a Sixteenth-Century Miller* (Baltimore: Johns Hopkins University Press, 1980); and Roger Bastide, *The African Religions of Brazil: Toward a*

Sociology of the Interpretation of Civilization (Baltimore: Johns Hopkins University Press, 1978). For a study of the process of appropriations of cultural manifestations of different social classes in Brazil, see Ruben George Oliven, *Violência e cultura no Brasil* [Violence and culture in Brazil] (Petrópolis: Vozes, 1989).

27. Interview with Luiz Carlos Barbosa Lessa on 4 October 1983.

28. Glaucus Saraiva, *Manual do Tradicionalista: Orientação geral para tradicionalistas e centros de tradições gaúchas* [Traditionalist manual: General orientation for traditionalists and centers for Gaúcho traditions] (Porto Alegre: Sulina, 1968), p. 51.

29. Sérgio da Costa Franco, "Pilchas," *Zero Hora*, 8 October 1985, p. 2.

30. Tau Golin, *A ideologia do gauchismo* [Gauchism ideology] (Porto Alegre: Tchê, 1983), p. 93.

31. Hugh Trevor-Roper, "The Invention of Tradition: The Highland Tradition of Scotland," in Eric Hobsbawm and Terence Regner, eds., *The Invention of Tradition* (Cambridge: Cambridge University Press, 1992), pp. 19, 22.

32. Antônio Augusto Fagundes, *Indumentária Gaúcha* [Gaúcho clothing] (Porto Alegre: Fundação Instituto Gaúcho de Tradição e Folclore); *Cadernos Gaúchos*, no. 2 (1977), p. 24.

33. Saraiva, *Manual*, pp. 57–58.

34. Luís Fernando Veríssimo, *O Analista de Bagé* [Analyst from Bagé] (Porto Alegre: L&PM, 1981).

35. *Regulamento da 11a Califórnia da Canção Nativa do Rio Grande do Sul* [Regulations for the Eleventh California for Native Music of Rio Grande do Sul], Article 10, paragraph 2 (Uruguaiana, 1981), p. 2.

36. Ibid., Article 15, p. 3.

37. Ibid., Article 1, p. 1.

38. Aparício Silva Rillo, Diogo Madruga Duarte, Juarez Fonseca, Luiz Carlos Borges, and Mauro Dante Aymone Lopes, *Carta de Uruguaiana* [Uruguaiana Charter] (2 November 1981), p. 1.

39. Ibid., pp. 1, 2.

40. Cícero Galeno Lopes, *A Anticarta de Uruguaiana* [The Uruguaiana AntiCharter] (Uruguaiana, November 1982) p. 2.

41. *Regulations*, Article 24, p. 6.

42. In the Fifteenth California, which took place in 1985, singers who had a Spanish accent were prohibited which caused much controversy since this festival takes place in Brazil, a city linked by a bridge to Argentina.

43. During the First State Congress on Culture, sponsored in 1989 by the Council on Cultural Development in the State of Rio Grande do Sul, in the Commission of Nativism and Folklore, a well-known traditionalist and folklorist decided to propose the submission to the General Assembly (which had deliberative power) the thesis that folklore is a "science that compares equally to the other social sciences." The reaction of the other traditionalists was at first cautious, thinking the topic was controversial and fearing the proposition would not be approved by the plenary group. Finally, another well-known traditionalist and folklorist whom I had interviewed noticed my presence and solicited "the view of the anthropologist." From being the researcher I became the research subject and suggested they present the proposal since they believed in it. I fur-

ther pointed out that, although I thought it would be approved, the recognition of its merit would only come about if folklorists had a greater productivity.

44. Juarez Fonseca and Gilmar Eitelvein, "Aiatolás da Tradição: Apontamentos para uma história natural" [Ayatollahs of tradition: Notes for a natural history], *Zero Hora*, Cultural Supplement, 14 June 1986, p. 8.

45. See Juarez Fonseca, "Aiatolás da tradição: Repercussões," [Ayatollahs of tradition: Repercussions], *Zero Hora*, Guide Supplement, 21 June 1986, p. 16.

46. Antônio Augusto Fagundes cited in Juarez Fonseca, "Os vira-bostas" [Cowbirds], *Zero Hora*, Guide Supplement, 26 March 1988, p. 12. In another interview, Fagundes affirms there is no nativism, a position that coincides with that of other members of the Gaúcho Traditionalist Movement for whom nativism is nothing more than a derivation of traditionalism. See his interview "Não existe nativismo" [Nativism does not exist], *Tarca Cultural Gaúcha 2*, no. 12 (March 1986).

47. Luiz Coronel, "Impasse ou conspiração?" [Impasse or conspiracy?], *Zero Hora* (27 May 1986), p. 4. In another article Coronel brings forth what amounts to a platform for the future: "It is necessary for a new wind to blow into our minds. If our power came from the sale of postcards, it would be enough to dress in folkloric garment. We need to sing of wells and hydraulics, carts, trains, planes, and space ships. Our power must come from our sweat over the land, from our intelligence, from our happily carrying out our actions. Instead of a dogmatic culture, we need an open culture that is critical and inventive. To be loyal to Rio Grande do Sul does not mean we are refusing the future. It is, above all, a commitment to it" ("Regionalismo: Impulso ou estagnação?" [Regionalism: Impulse or stagnation?], *Zero Hora*, 18 July 1986, p. 2).

48. Luiz Coronel was criticized by a traditionalist composer who accused him of "pretending to be a revolutionary, even politically. I want to suggest that his work (what he does in practice is what matters) is not at all revolutionary. His songs are actually extremely conservative" (Antônio Augusto Fagundes, "De Coronel a Silva Rillo" [From Coronel to Silva Rillo], *Zero Hora*, Guide Supplement, 7 June 1986, p. 6.

About the question of their poor taste, another polemic took place in 1984 with regard to the idea brought forth by the Rio Grandian Tourism Company which was adopted by the traditionalists. The suggestion was to transform into a large tea kettle and a gourd the two enormous cupolas at the entrance of the State Exhibit Park Assis Brasil, located in Esteio in the greater Porto Alegre area and used for agricultural exhibits. This park would then be called the "House of the Gaúcho." Many people and institutions, among them the Rio Grandian section of the Institute of Architects in Brazil, opposed the idea arguing that it was in poor taste. The architects, among whom the project was entitled "chimarró-drome," argued that it was an elementary and incorrect way to use state traditions, characterized by volume and disproportion (see "Casa do Gaúcho: IAB quer explicar caso" [House of the Gaúcho: IAB wants to explain the case], *Zero Hora*, 24 April 1984, p. 27. The traditionalists, on the other hand, condemned "the position of those who see in Rio Grandian traditions a symbol of all that is backward and retrograde. The greatest enemies of Gauchism are not abroad or in the center of the country; they are in Porto Alegre itself. In their puerile wish to appear cultured, advanced, modern, contrary to this rough behavior they seem to despise the smell of the people, too strong for their delicate nostrils. Yes, because it is not the people who are criticizing the idea but the elite. When one tries to remember some of its symbol, there is nothing of direct elections, now!" The people withdraw to their ignorance" (Antônio Augusto Fagundes, "Tradição e bom gosto" [Tradition and good taste], *Zero Hora*, 2d part, 28 April 1984, p. 10. The project never came to fruition.

49. Dilan Camargo, "O canto do passado" [The song of the past], *Diário do Sul*, 16 December 1986.

50. Araújo, "Sob o Signo da Canção," pp. 64–69.

51. "Uma Geração Nativista: A Pizza e a Coca-Cola cedem terreno para o carreteiro e o chimarrão" [A nativist generation: Pizza and Coca-Cola give way to carreteiro and chimarrão], *Tarca. Cultura Gaúcha* 1, no. 1 (1984): 4.

52. Dilan D'Ornellas Camargo, "Nativismo e tradicionalismo" [Nativism and traditionalism], *Tarca. Cultura Gaúcha* 1, no. 2 (1984): 11.

53. Araújo, "Sob o Signo da Canção," pp. 64–69.

54. The Cruzado Plan was an economic plan implemented at the beginning of 1986 by Brazilian President Sarney. The plan meant the creation of a new currency, the cruzado, to curb runaway inflation. It succeeded until the November 1986 elections and helped elect many candidates belonging to Sarney's party, the PMDB.

55. Antônio Augusto Fagundes, "Tradicionalista não vota em traditionalista" [Traditionalists do not vote for traditionalists], *Zero Hora*, Guide Supplement, 22 November 1986, p. 13.

56. *Carta de princípios do Movimento Tradicionalista Gaúcho* [Charter of principles of the Gaúcho traditionalist movement], in Saraiva, *Manual*, pp. 17–19.

57. Golin, *Ideology*, p. 12.

58. Tau Golin, *A Tradicionalidade na Cultura e na História do Rio Grande do sul* [Traditionalism in Rio Grandian culture and history] (Porto Alegre: Tchê, 1989), p. 46.

59. José Hildebrando Dacanal, "Ensaios Gauchescos I—Acertando as Contas com Jayme Caetano Braun" [Gaúcho essays I: Settling the account with Jayme Caetano Braun], *RS* (1–20 May 1990): 25; and "Ensaios Gauchescos II—Origem e Função dos CTGS" [Gaúcho essays II: Origin and function of the CTGS], *RS* (26–27 May 1990): 25.

60. José Hildebrando Dacanal, "Ensaios Gauchescos III—Tradicionalistas x Nativistas" [Gaúcho essays III: Traditionalists x nativists], *RS* (2–3 June 1990): 24–25.

61. See chapter 1 in this book.

62. See chapter 2 in this book.

6. New Frontiers in Culture

1. Néstor Garcia Canclini, *Culturas Híbridas* (Mexico: Grijalbo, 1989).

GLOSSARY

Abertura Opening. Period during the late 1970s and early 1980s when Brazil experienced a move toward democracy and the beginning of the end of the military regime.

Bandeirantes Flag bearers. Members of expeditions called *bandeiras* [flags] that between the sixteenth century and the beginning of the eighteenth century originated in the captaincy of São Vicente toward the backlands to enslave Indians and to search for precious stones.

Batuque Designates African religions in Rio Grande do Sul. Generic name for the music of percussion instruments usually associated with black culture in Brazil.

Bombacha Baggy pants traditionally worn by the Gaúcho.

California of Native Song Festival of Gaúcho music where composers enter a composition for the best traditional music composition of the year. It started in the city of Uruguaiana in 1971.

Campanha Grassland region of Rio Grande do Sul south of the Jacui and Ibicui Rivers and bordering on Argentina and Uruguay.

Candomblé African religions in the state of Bahia.

Caudilho Autocratic political leader who dominates his followers by force of his personality.

Chimarrão Another name for *mate*.

Chiripá Garment made up of a strip of material that goes between the legs and is attached to the waist by a leather belt.

CNPq [Conselho Nacional de Desenvolvimento Científico e Tecnológico]. National Council for Scientific and Technological Development.

Colono Colonist. Small land-owner of German or Italian descent.

CPC [Centro Popular de Cultura]. Popular Culture Center. Movement linked to the National Student Association that hoped to raise the consciousness of the popular masses through plays and other artistic forms. It was created in 1962 and ended with the 1964 coup.

Estado Novo [New State]. Name given to the dictatorship implanted by President Getúlio Vargas from 1937 to 1945.

FAPERGS [Fundação de Amparo a Pesquisa do Estado do Rio Grande do Sul]. Research foundation of the State of Rio Grade do Sul.

Farrapos Rags. Pejorative nickname given to Rio Grandian rebels between 1835 and 1845 by the imperial troops because of the condition of the clothes.

Farroupilha Diminutive of *farrapos* [rags]. Term designating the war between the state of Rio Grande do Sul and the Brazilian Empire, 1835–1845.

FARSUL Federation of Rural Association of Rio Grade do Sul, today the Agricultural Federation of the State of Rio Grande do Sul.

Gaúcho Rio Grandian; a person from the state of Rio Grande do Sul. Originally a pejorative word meaning "cattle thief" and later "ranch peon."

Gaudério Vagrant; vagabond.

Guasca Derived from the Quechua word *huasca*, meaning string or rope. A kind of cord made from raw cowhide. This was a term used in the past to designate the Gaúcho.

Intentona Comunista Communist uprising. Failed armed insurrection carried out by the Communists with the objective of taking over control in 1935.

Intervenors Those who governed the states during the Estado Novo. They were appointed by the president of the republic.

Invernadas Large fenced-off land areas used for fattening cattle.

ISEB [Instituto Superior de Estudos Brasilieros]. Institute for Brazilian Advanced Studies. Research entity created in 1955 and ended with the 1964 coup. It had a nationalistic orientation.

Mate Bitter tea drunk from a gourd through a straw. An emblematic symbol of the Gaúcho.

Medalhões Term used to designate people with power. Literally "big medals." Big shots.

Modernist Movement Initiated in 1922 in São Paulo to promote in Brazil artistic and intellectual updating with relation to Europe.

Tropicalist Movement Artistic movement that began in 1968 and was characterized by the appearance of new composers of popular music who were preoccupied as much with rhythm as they were with lyrics in showing the contrast between what was considered traditional and what was considered modern in Brazil. In doing so it revisited the preoccupations of the Modernist Movement of 1922.

Pampa Name given to the vast plains of the Gaúcho *campanha* as well as to a similar region in Argentina and Uruguay whose natural pasture lands are ideal for raising cattle.

Pilchas Typical suit of the Gaúcho including *bombacha*, boots, bandanna, and hat.

Piquetes Small groups of horsemen. A subdivision of the Centers for Gaúcho Traditions.

PMDB Partido do Movimento Democrático Brasiliero. Brazilian Democratic Movement Party. The party that successes the MDB (Movimento Democrático Brasileiro), the legal opposition party (1965–1979) during the military regime.

Prenda Literally a gift, an adornment. Designates the female partner of the Gaúcho.

República Velha [Old Republic]. Name given to the period from the proclamation of the Republic in 1889 until the 1930 Revolution.

Revolução de 1930 [1930 Revolution]. A movement begun by the lack of satisfaction of the peripheral oligarchies and that brought about the New Republic. This movement gave power to Getúlio Vargas, a political figure in the state of Rio Grande do Sul. He remained in power from 1930 until 1945 and later was president, from 1951 until 1954.

Sesmarias Land grants by the Portuguese crown. Each parcel of land measured thirteen thousand hectares.

SUDENE [Superintendência do Desenvolvimento do Nordeste]. Agency for the Development of the Northeast. Agency created during the 1950s to oversee and aid in the development of the Northeast.

Tenente Lieutenant.

Tenentismo Nationalistic reform movement and ideology of the military rebellions led by young officers in the armed forces during the 1920s.

UFRGS [Universidad Federal do Rio Grande do Sul]. Federal University of Rio Grande do Sul.

INDEX

Collective memory, 8
Collective unconscious: Gaúcho, 34
Colonists: German and Italian, xv,
79; German and Italian
descendants, 82–83
Colonization: Iberian, 38; Pampa
region, 54
Colono: meaning, 65
Communication: networks, 111
Communists: uprising, 26
Composers: nativists, 105
Comte, Auguste: small fatherlands,
57
Conflicts: ethnic and regional, 113
Constitution of 1988, 48
Consumer demand: Gaúcho cultural
products, 82
Convention: Santa Maria, 66
Coronel, Luiz: Gaúcho music, 106
Côrtes, Paixão, 93
Costume, 77
Council of cowboys, 62
Counterfeiting: cultural, 119n30
Country verse, 100–101
Coup: Third Army participation, 46
Cowbirds, 104
CPC, *see* Centro Popular de Cultura
(CPC)
Creole Flame, 59, 64, 71
Creole mass, 72
Creole wedding, 72
Crioulo: connotation, 127n10
Cruzado Plan, 108, 136n54
Culinary art: northeastern, 22
Cults: Afro-Brazilian, 85; Gaúcho, 72
Culture: borders, 3; diversity and
integration response, 116; hybrid,
115; identity and disappearance,
110; qualification, 69;
transmission, 67
Cultural Foundation of Curitiba, 78
Customs: inclusion of present-day,
57

Dacanal, José Hildebrando: Gaúcho
mythology, 110; Indian contribution, 40
Dances: Rio Grandian, 93

Dantas, Beatriz Góis: black culture,
84
Day of the Gaúcho, 58
Debt: state governments, 48
Decentralization, xii: administrative,
29; Brazilian, 16; objective, 5
Democracy: southern, 36
Demographics: skin color, 83
Department of Culture, Sports, and
Tourism, 71: objective, 75
Department of Education and
Culture, 71
Department of Gaúcho Traditions of
the Student Association: Júlio de
Castilhos Public School, 58
Department of Press and Propaganda,
26
Depression of 1929: consequences,
26
Deterritorialization: first steps, 79,
Gaúcho culture, 65
Discotheques, 81
Discourse: traditionalists and
nativists, 110–111
Diversity: twelve Rio Grandes, 34
Dorson, Richard M.: fakelore, 11–12
Douglas, Mary: *Purity and Danger*,
91
Dress: women in male garments, 98
Drummond de Andrade, Carlos, 18
Dundes, Alan: folklore study, 11
Durable goods, 28
Durham, Eunice Ribeiro, 9
Durkheim, Emile: totemism, 2–3

Eastern Europe, 113
Economics: abolition of borders,
113; denationalization, 29;
exploitation, 42; vitality, 47–48
Education, 26
Eleventh California, 100
Elitism: criticism, 21
Emigration: Rio Grande do Sul, 77
Entertainment: traditionalist
position, 66
Estado Novo, 26
Estrela, Antônio Carlos, 50
Ethnic minorities: culture, 25